The Catalog Showroom Formula

The Catalog Showroom Formula

J. M. de Bernardi

CHAIN STORE AGE BOOKS

An Affiliate of Lebhar-Friedman, Inc., New York

The Catalog Showroom Formula

Printing 5   4   3   2   1
Printed in the United States of America

Library of Congress Catalog Card Number: 73-92730
International Standard Book Number: 0-912016-30-2

To June

Contents

Preface

Every decade or so, a really new formula develops in the retailing field. To me, the *discount catalog showroom* has now joined these innovative ranks. The department store appeared (in Paris, France) in 1852 and was soon emulated around the world. Shortly after that, Aaron Montgomery Ward began selling through mail order. In 1879, Frank W. Woolworth came along with the variety store and was copied around the world. The "Woolworth of Australia" and the "Woolworth of South Africa" are not affiliated with the U.S. company. You see, even the name was copied.

In 1916, self-service changed food distribution. In the mid-1930s, the supermarket again added a new dimension to retailing. In 1955, the self-service, checkout department store appeared, incorporating the discount house pricing structure.

Discounting is not new. The catalog is not new. However, the way of selling by using the catalog, the showroom, and the discount pricing structure is *definitely* new. This is the reason for the excitement. No doubt the final ingredients for the discount catalog showroom are not yet mixed into the recipe. A new twist may still be yet to come. In the meantime, this book takes a look at what this new form of retailing is like and why it has come about—and what you should and should not do if you want to join in.

J. M. de Bernardi

The Catalog Showroom Formula

1

TV Time is Wishbook Time

The catalog—old and new. Who shops catalog
and why. Coded prices and the discount.

The catalog itself is nothing new. Montgomery
Ward and Company swings into Century 2 and Sears,
Roebuck soon will celebrate its centennial. In the days
of the horse and carriage, Macy's also did a very good
mail order business. The 1891 Macy's catalog had 311
pages. A few years later, the size of the catalog had
shrunk as Sears became the most powerful mail order
house. John Wanamaker was also very active in mail
order about this time. Of course, many department stores
throughout the country, including the prestigious Neiman-

Marcus, issue Christmas catalogs. Newspaper advertisements for department stores are miniature catalog pages in themselves as they call attention to how merchandise can be ordered by mail. So, the mail order catalog business has been part of retailing's picture for quite some time.

Early catalogs have been reprinted, and it is interesting to look at the drawings and the prices. However, the copy is also very fascinating. The 1915 Sears catalog starts off with the following:

> You may drive to town to get the price of wheat, or use the telephone—the modern way.
>
> You may write a letter to accept a price for a hundred acres of land and find the offer withdrawn before your letter arrives, or wire your acceptance and clinch the sale at once—the modern way.
>
> You may go to an average store, spend valuable time and select from a limited stock at retail prices, or have our Big Store of World Wide Stocks at Economy Prices come to you in in this catalog—the modern way.
>
> No matter where you live, rain or shine, you can with this catalog do your shopping from your easy chair. Consult its pages as your needs arise and you will experience the comfort and economy in buying that have made this Big Store the supply house of so many million homes—Buy the Modern Way.

The most modern maiden or young housewife *still* looks to the catalog for ready reference regarding price, quality, and sometimes even style. Although stores today are becoming larger, few can offer the selection offered by a catalog. Although there were some 1,676,800 retail stores [1] in the United States in 1973, the catalog still attracts.

However, the "modern way" of the catalog today includes a showroom—it is a combination of shopping from the catalog and buying in the showroom, at discount prices. And the buying was almost $1 billion in 1971, $1.5 billion in 1973, and it is estimated that it will be $5 billion in 1974. The number of discount catalog showrooms was about 1,500 in 1972 and is expected to be about 2,500 by 1975. [2]

The working wife especially votes for this system. The modern way for her is to "wish" at her convenience, either during the day when she wants to relax with that cup of coffee or at TV time. For the working wife, the catalog provides a basis for comparison shopping. When she needs a new coffee pot, a good place to start is with her "Wishbook." She not only gets the price but she is told about new developments in coffee pots, new features and finishes, and so on. The number of working wives in the United States is increasing:

> In 1945, there were about 15 million married women, and 7 million were working.
> In 1973, there were about 40 million married women, and 30 million were working.
> In 1980, there will be about 42 million married women, and 35 million will be working. [3]

---

[1] *U.S. Census of Business* and Conference Board.

[2] "Estimates on Catalog Biz: $1B to $1.5B," *Discount Store News*, Vol. 12, No. 16 (July 30, 1973), p. 1, and discussions with people in the field.

[3] U.S. Bureau of the Census, *Current Population Reports*, Series P. 23.

—An increase from 46.7 percent in 1945 to 83.3 percent in 1980 in the number of married women who are
working. As a matter of fact, it is not only married women
but very soon more than 50 percent of all women between
the ages of 18 and 65 will be employed.

At first, the working woman's style of living does
not change so much. Before long, however, she finds
she would rather participate in leisure-time activities than
do as much shopping as she did in her pre-employment
days. The catalog enters with great emphasis.

Young mothers who are forced to stay at home fol-
low the same pattern. Few will spend money on baby
sitters in order to comparison shop as frequently as they
did before they had children. Consequently, the catalog
is very important to them. Price is especially important,
but convenience becomes a prime factor in value. Sometimes, the customer will pay more if time is saved. Of
course, everyone prefers to get the best bargain.

When is a bargain a bargain? Apparently, in some
cases, time is a great value factor. The fast-food restau-
rants and the convenience food stores SAVE YOU TIME. Fast
in, fast out is the attractive feature. Everyone knows the
success stories of the Colonel and McDonald's fast-food
carry-outs. A similar story is there in the convenience
stores, too.

There are now about 18,000 convenience food stores
selling $3.750 million. Low prices here are traded for
fast in, fast out factor. For example, look on page 5 at the
margins in a convenience store and a supermarket.

The catalog and catalog showroom offer the fast in,
fast out factor, but the *discount* catalog showroom (DCS)
gives low prices, too. Catalogs—old and new—feature price
because the mail order houses know that customers like
to pick up, examine, and possess items rather than ex-

Gross Margins

	Convenience Stores	Supermarkets
Cigarettes	24%	6%
Beer	25	18
Soft drinks	21	17
Pet foods	19	4
Cereals	28	14
Juices	24	12

Source: "The Convenience Store Industry Report 1973," 4th Annual Study by *Convenience Store News,* pp. 8 and 9.

amine from a picture, order, and possess later. Therefore, a little compensation for this emotional delay is lower prices. The other comparison of the modern catalogs and the pre-turn-of-the-century one is that of discounting. Early catalogs featured very low prices. So do new ones. Aldens catalog says, "Inside this unusual catalog, you'll find many name brand items at EXCEPTIONALLY LOW PRICES!" The president, Carle Wunderlich, also says to me: "Dear Friend, if you think the prices in this catalog are suspiciously low, you're right. They are. But you can rest easy . . . there's method in our madness. Quite frankly, we're out to get 150,000 new customers. That's why we're willing to sell the merchandise in this catalog at prices close to our cost. . . ." Aldens has been for 84 years serving over 4 million American families.

I also have in front of me several DCS catalogs. Remember the D means "discount," so let us do some price comparison as the customer would do—either at break time or TV time.

First of all, we open the catalogs and usually find jewelry (particularly diamond rings). The 1895 Sears Catalog had 507 pages, of which 208 were for watches and jewelry. I have just finished counting the pages of several 1973 catalogs of various companies, and the ratio is very similar. It would be great (if we were watching television) to see a diamond commercial on television at this moment to whet our appetites, but few jewelry stores advertise via this medium. In any case, the presentation of diamonds in the catalogs is quite satisfactory. Most DCS's do a big portion of their business in jewelry, so naturally this is a feature item. To make a price comparison with the conventional catalogs—or with each other—is difficult, however. Mountings seem to be very similar, but the price varies a great deal for diamond rings. The importance of jewelry, however, is quite apparent.

The catalog format varies a great deal. Some are price coded; others list "our price" and "retail price." Volume Merchandising Co. features the coded price catalog, and its system is similar to most DCS catalogs. The coded price must be easily seen so that the difference between this figure and the retail figure can be noted at a glance. For example:

8976-1933x920 . . . . . Retail $15.00

would be listed under the item. *8976-1933* is the catalog order number (stock number). The *x* separates this number from the customer's price, which is $9.20.

The catalog can offer some specials, too. Although one of the features of the DCS operation is no markdowns, some items are highlighted as "specials." For example, Service Merchandise Company sent out a 48-page pre-Christmas catalog. This "seasonal" catalog had three or more "TRU-SPECIALS" on each page. In this case, the numbers following the so-called separation letter (usually *x* or *z*) are crossed out, and the new price is printed above.

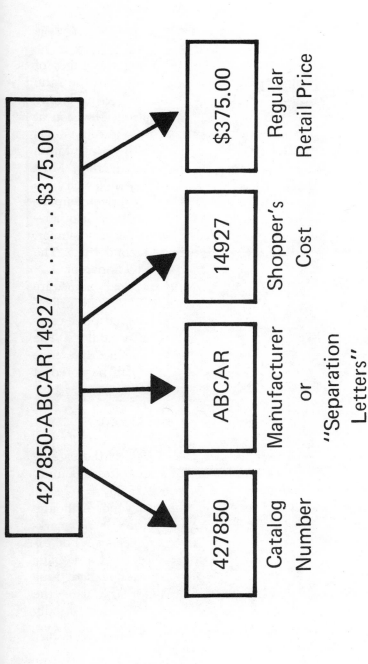

427850-ABCAR14927 . . . . **$375.00**

427850	ABCAR	14927	$375.00
Catalog Number	Manufacturer or "Separation Letters"	Shopper's Cost	Regular Retail Price

FIGURE 1 How to interpret the coded prices in most catalogs.

FIGURE 2 Part of a jewelry page showing "tru-specials" in the Service Merchandise pre-Christmas catalog.

In addition, the TRU-SPECIALS have the price in large numbers printed over or near the picture of the item on "sale." In this case, the termination date of this Christmas special was November 22, 1972. Obviously, this is to reduce the Christmas rush—which was indeed formidable during the 1972 holiday. Some managers said they did over 25 percent of their business between November 15 and December 25.

Most companies clear out-of-date or seasonal merchandise in these sale supplements usually about four times per year. In addition, the MacDonald Sales Center —a subsidiary of the E. F. MacDonald Company—advertises in local newspapers. The newspaper advertisement just before Mother's Day listed 16 items with illustrations. Bank Americard and Master Charge were shown in the ad.

Headlines included:

CHECK THESE ITEMS—PRICED BELOW LOW-LOW CATALOG PRICES

FOR THE GRADUATE. . . . . . FOR MOTHER

Boy Graduate. . .

Girl Graduate. . . .

In this MacDonald advertisement, the list price was shown, and then the new sales price was featured. At the top of the ad in a special inserted area is a photograph of the "Gift Catalog" saying "WITH CODED PRICE—SAVINGS ON 8,000 ITEMS." One further comment regarding price. The special sales price is very close to one-half the "list price."

Each of the "special" catalogs we are inspecting have

WE RESERVE THE RIGHT TO LIMIT QUANTITIES

notices featured on the front page. This is either for the benefit of the customer (sales promotion emotion) or there could be truth in the hint that the price to the housewife is lower than the price usually given to the dealer by the conventional wholesaler. Some of the catalogs indicate that the customer is in fact dealing with a wholesaler; others suggest that it is the manufacturer who has prepared the catalog. Actually, the manufacturers usually pay for the catalog, and "catalog coordinators" prepare it (see Chapter 2).

The catalog is not the same as trying on that $10,000 diamond ring in Tiffany's, but there is this matter of *threshold* resistance, which keeps many people out of such cathedrals of retailing.[4] As a matter of fact, one of the reasons that jewelry is a featured item is that *too many* people are kept out of jewelry stores on Main Street or the enclosed air-conditioned mall (EMAC) shopping center. Sales people are trained to keep an eye on those diamonds in the jewelry stores and, because of this rightful concern about customers' pilferage, there is a forbidding air in most conventional diamond shops.

The aim of the DCS catalog is to completely pre-sell the diamond customer (or any other customer, for that matter) through the catalog BEFORE she enters the store. Then, she comes in to examine it in the flesh and buys

---

[4] A customer "resists crossing the threshold" of some *too-elegant* fine stores thinking that the well-dressed salespeople will force him to spend more than he planned. The customer wants a $500 diamond and is afraid he will end up spending $1,000.

it with a minimum of fuss and loss of time. She saves money, and she saves time.

Few of the catalogs are over 500 pages. Most are in the 250- to 350-page category. The catalog coordinator does a selling job from the first page on (see Figures 3 and 4). For example, the following lines are all taken from the front pages of various catalogs:

> "We are proud to present for your buying pleasure your personal copy of our 1973 catalog."
>
> "Visit our Spacious showroom."
>
> "We maintain complete warehouse facilities making it possible for you to get the merchandise you want now."
>
> "Enjoy dependable service."
>
> "Buy with complete confidence."
>
> "Every article illustrated in this catalog is guaranteed."

So, the catalog and the showroom provide the best features of the mail order world and of the friendly store. In addition, the customer reads in the catalog that prices are subject to change without notice but they will certainly be decreased if costs decline.

Wage costs in the traditional jewelry store are about 10 percent (salespersons' salaries and bonuses only) but only 4 percent in the DCS jewelry section. Although the DCS has trained people in this section, it would be difficult to find every salesman who can state, for example, the story of diamonds, how to buy a diamond, the carat, color, clarity, cut, and so on in the perfect way that is listed in Volume Merchandising Co.'s *Concept '73* catalog or in any of several other catalogs.

concept '73

We are proud to present for your buying pleasure...

YOUR PERSONAL COPY OF OUR 1973 CATALOG. This catalog is designed and compiled especially for you. Look through this exciting new catalog offering more than 8,000 items for your personal use . . . . marvel at our exciting array of fine jewelry . . . . . our gift section . . . housewares . . . . appliances . . . . . electronics . . . . . sporting goods . . . . . juvenile furniture . . . .

VISIT OUR SPACIOUS SHOWROOM . . . . . where shopping is indeed a pleasure . . . . . eliminate the problems of crowds and parking, trudging from department to department or from store to store.

DISCOVER the outstanding collection of both popular and unique quality merchandise and LOWEST PRICES . . . . which are maintained throughout the year consistent with our policy to bring you name brand merchandise at the lowest possible prices every day.

INVENTORY TODAY Merchandise is available from our showroom. We maintain complete warehouse facilities making it possible for you to get the merchandise you want NOW.

ENJOY DEPENDABLE SERVICE Our trained sales personnel will be glad to assist you in every way possible in the selection of merchandise. Visit us soon and discover why our fine and enviable reputation is so well deserved.

FIGURE 3 The first page of Jewelcor's *Concept '73* catalog.

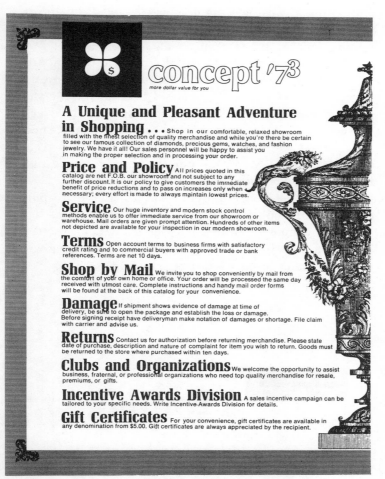

concept '73
more dollar value for you

A Unique and Pleasant Adventure in Shopping . . .
Shop in our comfortable, relaxed showroom filled with the finest selection of quality merchandise and while you're there be certain to see our famous collection of diamonds, precious gems, watches, and fashion jewelry. We have it all! Our sales personnel will be happy to assist you in making the proper selection and in processing your order.

Price and Policy
All prices quoted in this catalog are net F.O.B. our showroom and not subject to any further discount. It is our policy to give customers the immediate benefit of price reductions and to pass on increases only when necessary; every effort is made to always maintain lowest prices.

Service
Our huge inventory and modern stock control methods enable us to offer immediate service from our showroom or warehouse. Mail orders are given prompt attention. Hundreds of other items not depicted are available for your inspection in our modern showroom.

Terms
Open account terms to business firms with satisfactory credit rating and to commercial buyers with approved trade or bank references. Terms are net 10 days.

Shop by Mail
We invite you to shop conveniently by mail from the comfort of your own home or office. Your order will be processed the same day received with utmost care. Complete instructions and handy mail order forms will be found at the back of this catalog for your convenience.

Damage
If shipment shows evidence of damage at time of delivery, be sure to open the package and establish the loss or damage. Before signing receipt have deliveryman make notation of damages or shortage. File claim with carrier and advise us.

Returns
Contact us for authorization before returning merchandise. Please state date of purchase, description and nature of complaint for item you wish to return. Goods must be returned to the store where purchased within ten days.

Clubs and Organizations
We welcome the opportunity to assist business, fraternal, or professional organizations who need top quality merchandise for resale, premiums, or gifts.

Incentive Awards Division
A sales incentive campaign can be tailored to your specific needs. Write Incentive Awards Division for details.

Gift Certificates
For your convenience, gift certificates are available in any denomination from $5.00. Gift certificates are always appreciated by the recipient.

FIGURE 4 The second page of the *Concept '73* catalog, which is published by Jewelcor.

13

The catalog also gives other pertinent information regarding credit policies, mail orders, layaways, will-call, and so on. Even the weight is listed—and even the best salesperson in the world does not know this type of detail. Sometimes, the customer wants to know.

It could be said that impulse sales, often important sources of income to regular retail or discount stores, are decreased in the DCS. This could be true for the showroom where few samples are on display. However, in the catalog the presentation is beautifully done, and so the catalog is treated as a wishbook by the average customer. Not only can the item be seen but the explanation and usage is illustrated.

A dull television program or an idle hour plus a carefully laid out catalog adds up to DCS sales. If the customer cannot be drawn into the showroom, there is a phone number to call during the next TV commercial or an order blank to be filled out at that time.

2

Discount
Catalog Showrooms

A short definition of the *discount catalog showroom (DCS)*. DCS—What's in it? How it operates. Some statistics and operations guidelines.

An investor, an organization, or an independent individual looking for an opportunity in the new discount catalog showroom business could easily ask: What is it? What's in it for me? What do I do to do it?

The DCS is a special store with unique features. It is special because the system is a combination of clerk service, self-service, and checkout; part of the merchandise is readily accessible, and other items must be secured from the back room after selection is made from a catalog or from a one-only unit on display. Unique features include a coded price for customers, will-call possibilities, and even mail order. Let's investigate each of these points to determine WHAT IS IT? Let's start from the customer viewpoint.

The SYSTEM is service, self-service, and checkout. When the customer first enters the catalog showroom store, she may be required by some companies to pay a membership fee of $1.00 or $2.00 to be able to buy merchandise. She is given a card—and a catalog—and becomes a life member of this catalog showroom organization.

She walks into a store on the average of 8,000 square feet (although many new ones have 80,000 square feet). Before her, on supermarket-type gondolas, she sees— usually—housewares, small appliances, electronic items, and giftware. There are separate jewelry, toys, silver, and sporting goods areas. She may also see luggage displayed on gondolas. All these items are "one each." They are tagged with a store code (or vendor's code), the special numbers indicating the "secret" price and the retail price. The tag also says FOR DISPLAY ONLY. At the end of each gondola, there is a catalog desk or table with catalog, order blanks, and in some stores additional literature on how the system works or locations of sister units or perhaps a thank-you-for-shopping-with-us note asking for comments and suggestions.

The customer first selects an item from a catalog or from the display, and fills in the order blank with the following:

- Catalog number
- Quantity desired
- Short description
- "Secret" code
- Total prices (quantity desired times secret code)

Best Products Company, Inc
P. O. Box 26303
Richmond, Virginia
23260

Application for Showroom Purchase Card

COMPANY NAME _____
(please print)

APPLICANT'S NAME _____
First name   middle initial   last name

MAIL TO-ADDRESS _____
number   street

_____
city   state   zip code

NUMBER OF SHOWROOM CARDS DESIRED _____

SIGNATURE _____

Application is hereby made for a catalog and/or
showroom purchase card.
Misrepresentation, impersonation, or abuse of the privileges extended by
Best Products Company will result in cancellation of privileges
extended by Best Products Company.

PLEASE PRINT
Application for Catalog-Mailing list

$1.00 IS REQUIRED FOR APPLICATION TO HOME MAILING LIST

APPLICANT'S NAME _____
First name   middle initial   last name

MAIL TO-ADDRESS _____
number   street

_____
city   state   zip code

COMPANY NAME _____

SIGNATURE _____

FIGURE 5 Application for Best catalog and "membership" card.

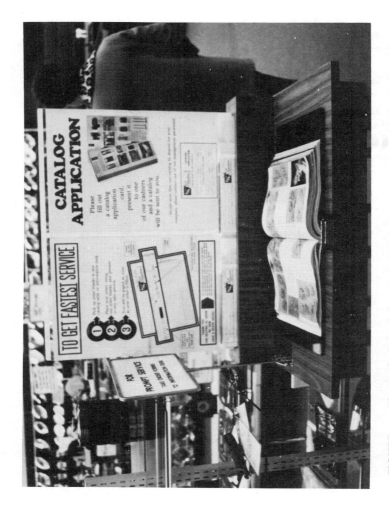

FIGURE 6 The end-of-gondola catalog desk; this one is in the Cincinnati, Ohio, Service Merchandise showroom.

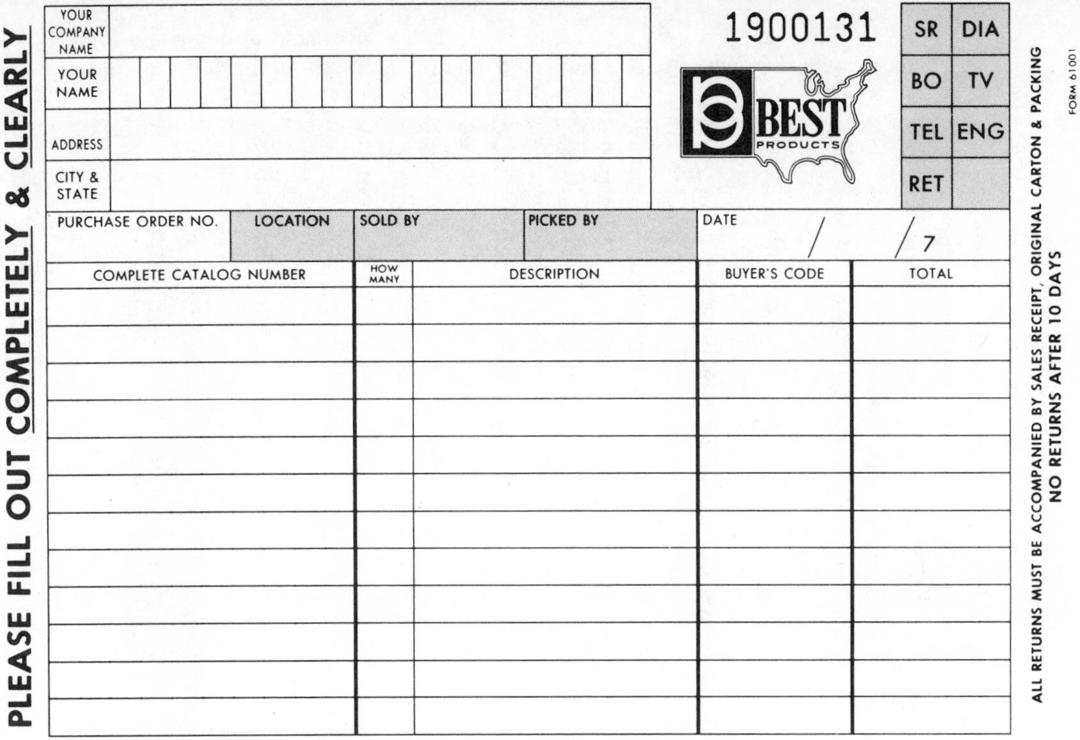
PLEASE FILL OUT COMPLETELY & CLEARLY

1900131

BEST PRODUCTS

SR	DIA
BO	TV
TEL	ENG
RET	

YOUR COMPANY NAME	
YOUR NAME	
ADDRESS	
CITY & STATE	

PURCHASE ORDER NO.	LOCATION	SOLD BY	PICKED BY	DATE / / 7

COMPLETE CATALOG NUMBER	HOW MANY	DESCRIPTION	BUYER'S CODE	TOTAL

ALL RETURNS MUST BE ACCOMPANIED BY SALES RECEIPT, ORIGINAL CARTON & PACKING
NO RETURNS AFTER 10 DAYS

FORM 61001

OTHER BEST LOCATIONS SHOWN ON REVERSE SIDE

FIGURE 7 The multi-copy Best order form.

The customer's name is listed on the blank. Some order forms may require a company name as well as address. Some DCS companies operate as if they were wholesalers or agents for businesses that need giftware for prizes in employee bonus programs. Consequently, there is space on forms for a company's purchasing agent and the company's address. There may also be a purchase order blank plus date, clerk's name, picked by, and other codes.

The customer next takes this order blank to the "information center" or service counter. Questions can be asked at this time of the personnel at this service counter who check the order blank. If the order is correct and filled in properly, the desk personnel send it by pneumatic tube or take it back to the warehouse. We will skip the warehouse operation and return to this part of the showroom store later on. When the order is filled, it is brought to a will-call point or customer pickup desk or counter with the original order. The order is taken to the cashier area and given to the cashier who calls out the name of the customer over the loud speaker. All this can take up to five minutes, but the system is geared to three-minute time frames.

This brings us to the other parts of the system. After the customer has turned in her order blank, she is free to wander around the rest of the store. She can select items from displays that are marked SELF-SERVICE and that also have tags that read "self-service item, please pay cashier" (rather than FOR DISPLAY ONLY). So, the customer can select something from one of these displays and continue her tour of the showroom. She could stop at the jewelry counter, ask a salesperson to see a diamond, select it, pay for it, and continue her tour. She could pass into the toys section or sporting goods section, which are in separate boutiques. In these sections, most items are

FIGURE 8 Interior of the Allentown, Pennsylvania, Jewelcor catalog showroom showing jewelry section and other "display only" areas. Courtesy of *Discount Store News.*

FIGURE 9 Self-service health and beauty aids section of the Evans Distributors and Jewelers showroom in Washington, D.C. Courtesy of *Discount Store News.*

on a regular self-service checkout basis, and she could select an item and take it to the checkout and pay for it. Then, when her name is called, she goes to the central or main bank of cash registers and pays for the display-only item plus any items selected on a self-service basis for which she has not yet paid. She pays and takes her merchandise or goes with a receipt to will-call, where she picks up the display-only merchandise. This tells us briefly what a catalog store is, at least from the customer's viewpoint.

What is in the catalog showroom store for the customer and the investor or operator? First the customer. So far, the automatic handling of merchandise and the low labor content involved permits the DCS to offer discount prices. This is interesting to the customer. The merchandise is usually national-brand merchandise that is not available at the conventional discount store. The customer also has the opportunity to select items at home before coming to the store, and this is important for expensive items such as silver and jewelry. Also, the DCS is new, and it is a shopping experience.

For the operator/investor, the investment is low. Why? One-item displays, back room mechanization, low wage costs, and so on. The net profits remaining after operations costs are high. Let us look at some of the reasons for this low investment and high return.

OFF-LOCATION, OFF-LOCATION, OFF-LOCATION. The original investment can be as low as one-half that of a regular discount store. One reason is that no glamorous location is required. They can be in out-of-the-way places because of the catalog. If the catalog is well presented, it will bring customers in to the store. THE LOOK CHEAP, BE CHEAP philosophy prevails although some of the DCS

FIGURE 10 Customer check-out area in Allentown, Pennsylvania, Jewelcor showroom. Courtesy of *Discount Store News.*

units are well designed and beautiful. Usually, all are located away from the new centers of retailing. Most are located on the fringes of warehouse areas or in cheap areas near major highways and expressways. However, some may be in shopping centers where rents (based on a percentage of sales plus minimum guarantee) are usually high (4 to 5 percent of sales). In Columbus and Dayton, Ohio, and St. Louis, Missouri, there are DCS units in neighborhood and community shopping centers because other retailers (such as Zayre and W. T. Grant) had moved out. This means that the shopping center owner is willing to take these second-generation occupants into the center at a lowered rental rate.

The usual procedure is for a DCS organization to build according to its prototype specifications on land either purchased or leased. Then, after completing the structure the DCS management sells the building or the entire property to a syndicate, bank, or insurance company, under the typical buy, build, and lease-back system. Recently, the DCS companies have been selling their properties to local professional men who need tax shelters. The large investment companies who previously handled most of the lease-back buildings have been requiring escalator clauses due to inflation, and this does not make the deal so attractive.

OPERATIONS produce a higher net profit also. The main reason is that the customer does the work of filling in the order and selection, which cuts back the requirement of high wages for store personnel. In addition, the catalog answers all the questions, yet the idea of service is presented through the personnel who are available if desired or needed. So, training costs are also low. Part-timers can be effectively used.

The fixturing and the inventory investment is not so high because there is a "warehouse" approach. The only area that is very well appointed is the jewelry section (and the silver room if this is also separate). Usually, the silver is merely behind locked glass doors along the walls of the major showroom area. A stack of merchandise does not have to sit on the sales floor—tying up inventory dollars. Rather, the computer determines the safety-stock level for the back room by season. It is less expensive to have merchandise in boxes in the back than beautifully displayed in the front end of the store. Less handling means lower wage rates.

In addition, control of merchandise means less SHRINKAGE from customers and employees. Both employees and customers must leave through specified doors. Store personnel must have proper receipts for all merchandise. Customers must have merchandise in boxes with receipts taped or stapled to the boxes. If pilferage is determined to be more than 1 percent (the maximum acceptable level), then mirrors can be installed in any blind corners and customers may also be required to check coats or shopping bags.

Shrinkage is reduced for other reasons, also. First of all, the expensive items are locked up and not accessible to either employee or customer. The U.S. government estimates that 7 percent to 10 percent of all business failures find their start in inside dishonesty. Official figures indicate that about $5 billion is lost to pilferage in retailing each year. Customer pilferage accounts for about 28 percent of this total; employee thefts, burglaries, vandalism, bad checks, and so on account for the rest. Many of the frequently used techniques in thefts by both employees and customers are thwarted in the DCS. For example, both customers and store personnel change prices on tickets. With the catalog pricing, this is not possible. The only time there is a price change is when there is markdown merchandise in the DCS. The markdowns in the DCS are a very small percentage. In department stores and specialty stores, the markdown figure is 6 to 8 percent of total sales. In conventional discount stores, it is 4 percent, and in the DCS it is only 1 percent.[1]

Some discount catalog showrooms use a clearance table for this markdown merchandise. Others have a red-tag or white-flag special. The Best Company's policy is to mark the merchandise down continuously for four weeks and then to give this merchandise to a local charity. Most of this merchandise is display items that have been damaged. The initial markdown is usually 25 percent. The second week, an additional 25 percent is taken and so on until the fourth week, when the price is very attractive. On this type of merchandise on this particular gondola, the price is changed by pencil by the manager and initialled. However, the amount of "clearance" items is small, and there is no problem in controlling the "unordinary" or lower-than-catalog-listed price.

Another way retail stores lose money is when an employee does not record merchandise. However, with the DCS order-blank system, the warehouse keeps a copy for inventory and re-ordering control, so there is both a real and a psychological reason for the cashier to ring up all merchandise. At the present time, the items on the self-service system do not comprise an important part of the business.

---

[1] Discussions with store management and *The Reid Report* (Chicago, Ill.: John E. Reid and Associates).

Unauthorized discounts are another form of thefts, but in the DCS, there are no "extra" discounts given to either employees or customers in most cases. The idea here is that the coded price is so much less than the listed retail price that an additional reduction could not be absorbed by the company. In fact, the reduction is substantial—25 to 40 percent below the regular price according to my comparison-shopping trips. There is legislation under consideration to remove this coded price technique from the formula. At the present time, there is tremendous impact in this method. Remember that early discounters were able to create the impact they did using this pricing method showing both "regular" and "discounted" price. They all selected items that the housewife knew and for which she could easily compare prices. Just in case she needed that extra punch, most early discounters showed two prices on the tickets: manufacturer's list price, $1.00, and "our" price, 69 cents, for example. Many discount stores and traditional retailers still use this method. So the customer, the operator, and the investor benefit from this new, more mechanized "automated" selling formula.

WHAT'S IN IT? Although it varies from store to store, the merchandise mix for the typical discount catalog showroom is as follows:

Jewelry	10 to 35%
Housewares and appliances	20 to 30%
Sporting goods	10 to 15%
Cameras and related items	10 to 15%
Toys	15%
Luggage and related items	5%

Source: As discussed with various DCS managements.

Ellman's Has Gem of Generator
For Profits in Jewelry

Ellman's of Atlanta has one of the strongest jewelry mixes in the catalog showroom industry. This is how the firm's sales and profits were generated, according to a prospectus for a recent stock offering:

Category	Sales	Profits
Diamonds, jewelry, watches	42.6%	55.3%
Leather goods, luggage, giftware, dinnerware, games	22.1%	19.7%
Housewares, hardware	11.8%	8.0%
Consumer electronics, traffic appliances, etc.	10.8%	7.8%
Camping, sporting goods, photography, musical instruments and optics	8.9%	6.3%
Linens, domestics, other soft goods	3.8%	2.9%

Source: *Discount Store News,* Vol. 12, No. 16 (July 30, 1973), p. 28.

The next "what" is WHAT DO I DO TO DO IT? There are several ways already tested, being tested, or being discussed as the formula becomes an established one. These include:

- The independent independent
- The chain operation by an established retailer such as
  Grand Union
  Vornado
  Mammoth Mart
  Giant Stores

Giant Food
Zayre
Kings

- The catalog operators who expand into showrooms (and there are several of these)
- The combination (May and W. T. Grant's and other joint ventures for example)
- The franchise
- Other combinations guided by the discount catalog showroom coordinator

The INDEPENDENT INDEPENDENT is usually the way a formula starts. The discount catalog showroom is closely related to the discount stores, and we will cover this point later. The independent usually has guts, however, and very little to lose by trying a new formula. In the DCS case, it is matter of securing a site, securing merchandise, and printing a catalog. The Midwest seems to be a spawning ground for innovations in the catalog showroom business. The location can be almost any building anywhere *if there is no congestion during evenings, Saturdays, and Sundays.*

No PARKING—NO BUSINESS is a statement that holds as true for the DCS as it does for the supermarket. Of course, highly populated areas are the exception. In any case, low rent is important and a fancy building is not a requirement.

A fancy catalog is important—it is advertising, and color is a must for jewelry. The merchandise can be secured through wholesalers, jobbers, manufacturer's representatives, and so on. The very small independent may work with a few large vendors and suppliers. The catalog can be printed by the independent with some assistance (financial plus photographs and layout) from the manufacturers or vendors. Every aspect of the business continues in this very individualistic or homemade way.

Obviously, the chains and franchise operations as well as combination ownerships cannot operate at this special level. Starting with the building and site itself, a certain prototype must be followed because it would cost more to deviate from the established formula than would be saved in rents. Procedures must be followed to produce the economies of scale for the larger companies.

In the case of a franchisor, there must be procedures so that guidance is meaningful.

Flexibility is permitted, however, and some new buildings have a second-floor warehouse over the showroom; others have a basement warehouse under the showroom. The same type of equipment to handle the flow of merchandise to the showroom cashiers from the warehouse is utilized and adapted so that here, too, some mass purchases can be made and new systems design is not required.

The most important factor in the complete DCS warehouse facility, as in any warehouse, is *control*. Inventories must be accurate so that safety-stock levels are maintained. This is very important to the DCS formula because of the number of "for display only" items. Out of stocks seemed to be a common problem during the 1972 Christmas season, and this is one sure way to gain dissatisfied customers. According to a *Discount Store News* vest-pocket survey, 26 percent of the DCS customers interviewed complained about out of stocks (see pages 45–47). This control factor is one very important reason for the multi-copy order form. This factor is also why many discount catalog showrooms, including Giant

Food, are beginning to use point-of-sale terminals for computerized inventory control. Of course, Giant has the experience from its supermarkets for this mechanization, but as your operation grows larger, it is something to consider. Whether computerized or not, your warehouse must be organized so that when the clerks send back the order form, the warehouse personnel can go to the picking board, find the location for the item on order easily, pick the item quickly, and send it up to the will-call desk. Remember, we said that this operation was geared to three-minute time frames. If the picking board is not well coded or if the inventory is in the wrong picking slot, the customer will be finished with her self-service tour and will be waiting.

Merchandise and catalogs of the various independents and chain operations—no matter how they are connected to each other (franchisor, coordinator, chain headquarters, showroom operator, and so on—are suspiciously similar. The reason is that manufacturers oversee and underwrite the catalog and the merchandise selection, working with buying groups and coordinators who are extremely professional. At the time of this writing, there are only 16 catalog coordinators who service almost all the showrooms in operation (see page 36). So, there is bound to be a great deal of overlap in the catalogs.

OTHER VARIATIONS. Independents can join other advisory groups, the trade association (the new National Association of Catalog Showroom Merchandisers—formed in 1972), plus the cooperatives. There are cooperatives in the wholesale field (both food and nonfood), and the catalog showroom fits into this category. Each independent is actually a part owner of the cooperative. Each member elects officers and the operating members or operations committee, who are dedicated full time to the

FIGURE 11 Picking board in the back room warehouse of Service Merchandise's Cincinnati, Ohio, showroom. Merchandise locations are listed by vendor, showing bin and shelf position.

33

operations of the company. Profits are divided among the members or returned to the business. Very often, each independent must own the same number of shares. If this is not the case, profits are prorated depending upon the shares owned.

The operations committee is a professional group hired by the cooperative's executive committee or Board of Directors if this is the type of structure employed. This professional group is the communications link between the vendors, suppliers, or manufacturers, and the members of the cooperative. It is up to the members of the cooperative to decide if there is to be a complete warehouse facility or if there are to be freight transfers only (in and out warehousing) for shipping charges savings— or if it will run on drop shipments only. In addition to the actual supplying of merchandise, the operations group studies various problems of the catalog preparation and catalog showroom operations, location, financing, and other problems.

The cooperative helps members determine sites, equipment, investment, and actual operations details. This could apply to new members or to members who wish to expand. A new member benefits from all the services upon payment of the membership costs, which are the shares in the corporation. A real benefit to this new member is the opportunity to exchange ideas not only with the professional staff but also with other members of the cooperative. Usually, there is a system whereby a member or team from the cooperative headquarters spends one week with the new member in establishing procedures if the site is already decided. Then, an additional week is spent by the new member at another cooperative member's showroom in order to see how the system works and in order to gain actual experience.

Usually, the membership meets at least once a year. Very often, there is a meeting each time a catalog is being prepared so that members can attend shows and exhibits in connection with the catalog and merchandise. Each member chooses the pages (and consequently the merchandise) he wishes to offer for sale. Because most catalogs are prepared by the coordinators, most of these "buying shows" are run by the coordinators. The flexibility that each coordinator allows its subscribers in selecting or customizing its catalog varies. At these meetings, the manufacturers (suppliers, vendors, and so on) sponsor seminars and instructional meetings on personnel handling, advertising, decoration, cleanliness, security, and so on. At this time, the suppliers also offer their assistance in the preparation or the cost of the catalog.

In any case, there is help from several quarters for the inexperienced or the experienced retailer who wishes to enter or expand the catalog (discount) showroom business.

We have already mentioned the catalog coordinators —the catalog publishers—and the fact that most showroom operators buy their catalogs and therefore their merchandise from them. Coordinators do offer varying degrees of service to their subscribers. These range from Giant Food, which just sells its catalog and leaves obtaining the merchandise up to the operators (this discourages people with no general merchandise background), to the majority of coordinators who sell the books and participate in obtaining the merchandise, to coordinators such as Mutual Merchandising, which publishes a detailed Product Information book. This is compiled annually and contains sources for merchandise, shipping weights and costs, credit terms, discounts, shipping times, and other information a showroom operator might need about obtaining the merchandise in the Mutual catalog. Below is a list of the catalog coordinators in this country, ranked by size from largest to smallest in terms of number of showrooms they serve.

- Creative Merchandising & Publishing, Inc., Minneapolis, Minnesota
- Mutual Merchandising Co., New York, New York
- Progressive Buying Associates, New York, New York
- American Merchandisers, Minneapolis, Minnesota
- Jewelcor (formerly Srago Associated Catalogs, Inc.), Miami, Florida
- Paul Schultz Catalog, Inc., Louisville, Kentucky
- Comprehensive Merchandise Catalogs, Inc., New York, New York
- Merchandisers' Association, Inc., Chicago, Illinois
- Federated Merchandising, Chicago, Illinois
- Dahnken Co., Salt Lake City, Utah
- ARM Distributors, New York, New York
- DLI, Kenmare, New York
- Warren Abbey Co., Inc., Cleveland, Ohio
- Charter Catalog, Atlanta, Georgia

Creative Merchandising is the biggest publisher (5 million books in 1973) and has an estimated volume of almost $6 million. Jewelcor was very active in 1973, selling its book to retailers new to the catalog showroom field, and it plans to print 5 million books in 1974.[2] DLI is one of the newest, having started in 1970; and Charter

[2] *Discount Store News*, Vol. 12, No. 16, pp. 15 and 18.

Catalog, formed by a group that broke away from Jewelcor, started in 1973. Giant Food also broke into the coordinator business in 1973, with three other chains using its book for the first time in the fall.

According to a *Discount Store News* report,[3] the formation of Charter Catalog (the split was made because the Charter members wanted to feature more jewelry than Jewelcor did) and Giant Food's step into the role of coordinator are not isolated incidents but rather the beginning of a trend. This trend will be either a "proliferation of coordinators" or a growing number of showroom operators producing their own catalogs. The *DSN* report saw this trend resulting from two factors: The individual demand for specialized catalogs that fit the merchandising needs of individual markets, which cannot be satisfied by "universal catalogs" or package options; and the saturation of key markets by major catalogs, which can lead to two adjacent showrooms using the same book. Merchandisers' Association, Inc. (MAI), among others, tries to give its members a stronger influence over what goes into their catalogs by having a merchandising committee for each of its big merchandise categories. Progressive Buying Associates is committed to protecting its members from head-to-head competition by not signing up new members in existing members' markets. However, this is not the usual procedure, and with the rapid growth of the catalog showroom business, this type of competition is inevitable unless more coordinators do guarantee exclusive markets.

[3] "New Trend Seen: A Proliferation of Coordinators," Vol. 12, No. 16, pp. 11 and 38.

3

The "D" in DCS

Again, how important is the discount? What about competition from the SSDDS (self-service, discount department stores)? Are the two complementary?

"Poor people need low prices, rich people love low prices." (Folk wisdom) "It's smart to be thrifty." (Macy's) "The cheapest supply house on earth." (Sears) The 1895 Sears catalog says that a 3 percent cash discount will be allowed when payment in full accompanies the order. That leads us to the all-time question, "How important is the discount?" What will the DCS do to the SSDDS? Maybe nothing—maybe everything.

The February 26, 1973, issue of *Discount Store News*,

in an article on page one, shows the experiment of Zayre.
The following is a quote from this feature:

> Zayre, lingering on the threshold of the catalog
> showroom industry, is experimenting with in-store de-
> partments that are structured so similarly to actual cata-
> log showrooms that only the catalog is missing.
>
> The mechanics of the experiment, which have been
> closely guarded by Zayre since their implementation in
> about eight stores last October, deviate so widely from
> the chain's traditional self-service pattern that the test
> can only be defined as a flirtation with the showroom
> concept.
>
> The experimental department, as surveyed by *DSN*
> in Zayre's store here in the northern fringes of the
> Albany market, consists of eight 20-ft. gondolas of floor-
> sample merchandise. As in catalog showrooms, customers
> write up their own orders and collect and pay for mer-
> chandise at a pickup desk.
>
> Zayre is merchandising a mixed-bag selection of
> giftware through the 13,000 sq. ft. test department. The
> 'catalog' department is in no way segregated from the
> rest of the store, except that goods are displayed on glass
> shelves instead of the metal and plastic gondolas used in
> the rest of the unit.
>
> Wall signs in the department explain procedures to
> customers. The clerk at the pickup desk, which faces the
> department, also is eager to detail the workings of the
> area to shoppers.
>
> Simply, a customer browses through the depart-
> ment until she finds a satisfactory piece of merchandise.
> She then selects a stock order form from one of the pads
> connected by a wire to each gondola run. The item,
> Zayre style number and color of the merchandise are
> copied by the customer from the price tag onto the order
> form.
>
> Completed forms are presented at the pickup desk

to the clerk, who then retrieves the selected item from
an adjacent stock area. The customer pays the clerk, is
given the receipt portion of the order form and leaves the
store without passing through the central checkout.

Price tags in the 'catalog' department list a 'comparable price' as well as the 'Zayre discount price.' A
typical item, a fondue set, had a 'comparable price' of
$19.50 and a 'Zayre discount price' of $16.87.

The eight gondolas, which are converted into 16
sides, are used to display non-branded giftware, most of
which is carried in the housewares and traffic appliance
departments of Zayre stores not participating in the experiment. But, 20 running ft. of silverware is not duplicated in most other Zayre units.

On page three of the same issue of *DSN*, we read the
headline that "U.S. Discounters Rated Second to European Cousins." The article is referring to the aggressive-
ness of Carrefour (discount stores with mammoth square
footage)—and indicating that the SSDDS in the United
States is growing at a declining rate and more open to
price competition. Let us take a look at the Carrefour
organization.

The Carrefour operation comprises approximately 50
hypermarkets [1] in France, Belgium, Switzerland, England,
and soon in Scotland, Canada, and Martinique. Sales are
approaching the $500 million mark at a very rapid pace.
Carrefour was founded in 1959 by two families—one had
food stores and the other a department store. The hypermarket has food and nonfood items sold behind one set
of checkouts. The SSDDS in the United States usually has
two sets of checkouts because the food department is
usually a concession. The idea for the hypermarket formula

---

[1] *Hypermarché* or hypermarket is the 100,000 to 200,00
square foot one-stop shopping, self-service, checkout discount store.

came from the early U.S. discounters and is now being "re-imported."

For example, after more than two years of study, The Jewel Companies have opened a Grand Bazaar in Chicago. It consists of 105,500 square feet—89,000 square feet for a Jewel supermarket and 16,500 square feet for an Osco drug store, which sells everything from 66 cent battery testers to full-size vacuum cleaners and $300 stereos. However, there are separate checkout banks for the supermarkets and the drug store.[2]

The first Carrefour store was a small supermarket at the intersection of two roads in Annecy, France. Hence, the name *Carrefour*, which means "intersection of two roads" in French—as well as in English (Webster's Collegiate Dictionary, page 124). It had about 6,500 square feet—a far cry from the present-day, huge stores.

The key to Carrefour's success may be in M. Marcel Fournier's, the owner-founder, philosophy:

> **"Experience is a brake—**
> **Heritage is a servitude—**
> **Organization is an iron collar."**

Each store is supplied independently and merchandise is not processed through a central warehouse. The stores are either company owned and operated, or franchised. The franchise system is similar to our own, but the re-imported model is more of an individual. The following chart indicates that the hypermarché in Europe enjoys a better operating posture than its U.S. counterpart:

[2] "Oo-la-la! Jewel Unveils Store Patterned on Hypermarche," *Discount Store News*, Vol. 12, No. 23 (Novmber 5, 1973), pp. 1 and 49.

	Carrefour (and Similar European Operations)	USA Discount Store
(Food/Nonfood combined)		
Gross Margin	14.25%	28.83%
Wages	6.52%	11.45%
Maintenance	1.71%	1.61%
Advertising	0.25%	1.95%
Gross Profit Before Tax	3.43%	2.98%
Average Sales	$10.90	$8.60
Stockturns	16 per year	8 per year
Terms of payment to suppliers	45 days	10 days to 3 months
1973 Average Size (total)	130,000 sq. ft.	75,000 sq. ft.
Parking	1,800 cars	750 cars
Sales	$11,000,000	$5,100,000

The Carrefour store at Marseille is 213,000 square feet.

Source: *Discount Store News,* Vol. 12, No. 5 (February 26, 1973), p. 3, and discussions with Carrefour operators.

Carrefour, Montesson—An Example

Land	635,000 sq. ft.
Parking	1,300 cars
Selling Space	76,000 sq. ft.
of which	30,000 for food
	21,000 textile
	15,000 hardgoods
	10,000 miscellaneous
Stockroom	42,500 sq. ft.
Offices	19,700 sq. ft.
Cash Registers	40 NCR class 5 with tape
Gasoline	12 pumps
Restaurant	274 seats
Total Personnel	350 people

Source: Figures taken on my visit to store.

Although it is difficult to compare the U.S. discount stores with Carrefour because of this nonintegration of food items in the United States, the above figures could indicate that the SSDDS here may have lost its feel for "warehouse selling" and has become a department store. Warehouse selling is returning to the pile it high, sell it cheap philosophy. The new adaptation can be seen in furniture distribution—at stores such as Levitz and Wickes.

The largest Carrefour stores are over 200,000 square feet and have 70 NCR checkout machines lined up at the entrance to the store. However, the mini-EMAC concept is well utilized. In addition to the very large discount store, there are several small boutiques off the main aisle outside this central checkout and leading either to it or away from it. I have studied a similar concept in other countries. So far, our DCS units have no food or boutique areas, but the separated toy sales areas indicate tremendous possibilities.

The large size of the Carrefour units permits the display of merchandise in warehouse containers or on some type of pallet. Fork-lift trucks are also employed right on the floor of the store. The *pile it high, sell it cheap* concept lives on. Both the SSDDS and the DCS have become space conscious and more luxurious than any early discounter would have dared.

Discount Store News has reported that the DCS hurts "old-liners" more than discounters. For example, DSN has published the following:

> Conventional department stores are feeling the impact of the catalog showroom boom more than the discounters, according to a recent DSN vest-pocket survey conducted in Northern New Jersey.
> However, the appeal of pre-planned shopping at

home and lower prices on small traffic appliances seem to be having some effect on both types of consumers as evidenced by the fact that 45% of those interviewed (14 of 31) said they are shopping less in conventional and discount department stores since they began catalog shopping.

A full 100% of the customers interviewed at Grand Union's Grand Distributors showroom here, and the Sutton Place showroom in Rahway, New Jersey, expect to return for future purchases.

Some 60% of those questioned (18 of 30) split their shopping evenly between conventional and discount retailers, but another 33% shop primarily in conventional stores while only 7% shop mainly discount. The normally high-line consumer apparently feels the catalog concept offers him an opportunity to buy quality, brand-name items at discount, or below, prices, and he is attracted by the sedate and orderly display appearance within the showrooms.

Although many customers indicated they are willing to 'go out of my way' to shop at a catalog showroom, 35% of those questioned (11 of 31) did express some criticism of the operation. Complaints about out-of-stock items were especially prevalent with 26% (8 of 31) of the customers voicing a gripe.

As mentioned before, lower prices on small electrics and the convenience of shopping at home are the main selling points in the recent showroom boom. Fully 77% of those interviewed (24 of 31) mentioned the two points as prime considerations in their showroom shopping; 26% were impressed by displays and the showroom layouts.

Both of the showrooms visited measure approximately 12,000 sq. ft. in display area, have been open only since last fall, and are located in relatively busy shopping areas. Grand Distributors has expanded the typical showroom concept by carrying certain stationery supplies, including greeting cards. The Sutton Place operation (a Two Guys offspring) allocates sizable space to home entertainment.

If consumer habits are changing, and 52% of those questioned (16 of 31) said they have noticed a change, it is primarily in the areas of traffic appliances and gifts which are pulling in most of the catalog customers, despite the concentration on jewelry.

'I don't do as much store-to-store shopping as before,' one customer said. 'If I need a small appliance or a gift I'll check out my catalog at home to see if the showroom carries it. I find I am shopping less in other-type stores for these particular items.'

Of those interviewed, some 80% (24 of 30) successfully purchased what they came into the store to buy, and the rest either bought something else or left the showroom empty-handed. While most customers enter a showroom with pre-set notions of what they intend to buy, 55% of those interviewed (17 of 31) indicated a willingness to browse and buy on impulse.

About 45% of those questioned (14 of 31) said they shop in conventional or discount department stores at least once a week; 42% (13 of 31) said they have shopped in other catalog showrooms, and 65% (20 of 31) had shopped in that particular showroom three or more times.

The 31 DSN interviews at the two North Jersey showrooms mentioned above are summarized in the following table. My own interviews with shoppers and owners over the past couple of years confirm these figures.

Divide shopping between discount and conventional
  department stores 60%
Shop in some conventional stores 90
Shop primarily in conventional stores 33

Shop in some discount stores 67%
Shop primarily in discount stores 7
Customers who will return to shop in a catalog
    showroom 100
Were able to purchase what they came into the
    catalog showroom for 80
Are shopping less in other stores 45
Complained of out-of-stock items 26
Shop in other catalog showrooms 42

When we look at the list of those companies who have entered the DCS business, we must agree with *DSN* that the conventional stores are indeed very interested in this development. We must look very closely at objectives and motives before stating that the discount catalog showroom is complementary to the discounters and is taking business away from traditional outlets. There had to be a good reason for Giant Stores to take its Summit catalog service desks out of its discount units; and although Grand Union's catalog branch, Grand Distributors, will be opening alongside a company supermarket, it minimizes duplication of merchandise with the company's discount Grand Way units. Grand Way executives have the authority to lower their prices whenever Grand Distributors seems to undersell them on items that are duplicated.

On the other side of the coin, the DCS operators must watch the hypermarkets carefully because they come the closest to the catalog showroom formula—only the book is missing. If coded prices are abolished, the pricing advantage of the DCS might be gone, also.

4

Something for Everywhere and Everyone

The discount catalog showroom has some grandparents still alive. A look at how the very early discounter operated. There are still some of the early 5 percent shacks. Each offers something to a certain customer. The customer segmentation principle is applied. Locations are everywhere.

This chapter could be one line: THE DISCOUNT CATALOG SHOWROOMS LOCATE ANYWHERE AND EVERYWHERE.

Want to open a DCS? Anywhere (seemingly) is fine. But some do better than others. Some of the very early discount operators that opened in abandoned factories, closed warehouses, barns, and garages are still in business.

Check your own thinking. Isn't that old place still doing business down by the railroad tracks? And isn't it fun to go out to the old barn (an actual barn, now expanded of course) once a year or more often to poke around? In the discount field also, the little hole in the wall that had a catalog in 1948 sold you the merchandise cash and carry for 5 percent above cost. Sometimes they would even show you the invoice. Something for everyone can apply in a country with 210 million people. There is no disputing (or discussing perhaps) taste. Cicero said it so well about 2,000 years ago.

However, we can look at some facts and see where some of the old and new and forthcoming DCS units will be located. Emphasis must be placed on the NO PARKING—NO BUSINESS principle for almost every location. New York City and similar center locations are exceptions. However, W. Bell in Washington, D.C., has just consolidated locations. Parking (and traffic congestion) seem to be one of the reasons.

You should test your early formulas in existing buildings. This is a rule because expenses must be kept low as your initial, experimental formula might not work out. But then new buildings are constructed on the basis of your tested, successful formula. This was true for the old John Wanamaker store in Philadelphia. Perhaps the first *real* "department store" saw its beginnings in this old Pennsylvania Railroad freight depot at 13th and Market Streets (May 6, 1876, was the grand opening). It is also interesting to note that Wanamaker's "Mail Order Bureau" started in a 9 x 12 room in 1876. And how this depot grew . . . into the great cathedral of retailing in Philadelphia.

Guidelines are yet to be established as can be seen

by the following piece entitled "Everyone should have such problems."

> Catalog showroom operators have yet to arrive at optimum size and site standards. The industry's still so young that sizes range all over the lot—from under 10,000 square footers to 50,000 sq. ft. and above units. There's also been much site experimentation, with units cropping up next to supermarkets, adjacent to home building supply stores, as freestanding units and even in shopping centers. One chain, New Jersey-based Supermarkets General, is trying its Valu House catalogers in a number of sizes—from 10,000 sq. ft. to 50,000 sq. ft.—and a variety of siting arrangements. The trouble is, all the units (except for the center Valu House which has not yet opened) have been apparent successes, and Supermarkets General is still stuck with the same problem it had before; finding an optimum size and site arrangement.[1]

However, some of the checklist below cannot be ignored. We have already mentioned parking but there is also

- Zoning
- Expansion possibilities
- Congestion problems (both pedestrian and vehicular)
- Neighbors and competitors
- Quality of surrounding customers (income)
- Population mix (age, buying habits)

[1] *Chain Store Age Executive Edition,* June 1973, p. E6.

- Nearby tenants
- Desired market image and customer segmentation regarding advertising policy

In addition to opening in these empty factory-type buildings, discount catalog showrooms are the second generation tenant of many small (neighborhood) and community (middle-size) shopping center stores.

Then, there are the conversions and switches. Shoppers Fair stores have become discount catalog showrooms owned and operated by another company. This is true for Zayre units that have become Service Merchandise showrooms. In addition, there are companies that have not been pleased with a self-service discount department store or discount supermarket operation and have converted to a discount catalog showroom. The Pathmark that has become a showroom in Paramus, New Jersey, comes to mind as an example.

The famous GEX experiment in Buffalo, New York, is another type of location (and is similar but not completely so to Giant Food, Inc., in Washington, D. C. Giant Food does not have all the merchandise out as does GEX). GEX says:

> "Now you can also browse and shop at home with our beautiful discount catalog and then come into our Catalog Showroom and purchase the merchandise you've selected. If you prefer, you may order your merchandise with the order blank found in the back of this catalog."

So, GEX's showroom is a store within a store. This type of catalog operation could be a tremendous addition for a corporation such as Zale. Already, this company has several discount catalog showrooms operating under the

O. G. Wilson name. A look at Zale's annual reports shows they have about:

- 1,000 jewelry operations
- 316 footwear units
- 69 drugs and sundries shops
- 20 sporting goods units
- 10 home furnishing stores
- 5 toy operations
- 150 softgoods units

Annual sales for Zale are $500 million and net profits are at the $25 million mark. This could have a very dramatic effect on the expansion of the DCS if Zale were committed to adding many locations. We are reminded that the Great Atlantic & Pacific Tea Company shifted from small service units to large supermarkets in the late 1930s. In 1931, A&P had over 15,500 small shops. By the end of the decade, thousands of these had been closed and larger supermarkets opened in different locations (the off-locations similar to the DCS today). Today, the 4,250 A&P units are large supermarkets. In any case, thousands of small retailers as well as the larger companies are looking at the new DCS developments. Suburban-located stores perhaps are not so threatened as the downtown stores that are being hit once more. First it was the supermarkets, then the shopping centers, then the discount department stores, and now the catalog showrooms.

A LOCATIONS SUMMARY. Putting all this together, we can say that some discount catalog showrooms are operating well in downtown, warehouse areas, and off-locations. However, almost all the new ones are in suburban locations not too far from the shopping centers and new centers of distribution and retail trading. Future locations might be the gasoline stations that seem to be closing in great numbers. If Cleveland, which has a heavy concentration of DCS units, is any barometer of the future, showrooms now in downtown locations will be moving out into the suburbs—not just adding additional units there. For example, Esco has closed its two inner-city units and opened four suburban sites. *Discount Store News* quoted a U.S. Merchandise spokesman, who was explaining his company's exodus to the Cleveland suburbs, as saying, "Our market has always come from the suburbs. It's just a matter of us moving closer to our customers." [2]

- A DCS in downtown New York city comprises an exception.
- There are a few DCS's in built-up locations.
- Modern Merchandising units are in suburbs.
- Best is building in the suburbs in very fine buildings.
- Service Merchandise is in former discount department store locations but building in solo locations along suburban roads (and in Cincinnati near an Interstate and close to an enclosed mall).
- E. F. MacDonald has made no complete future commitment but seems to be sold on the suburbs, too.
- The Giants are in the suburbs.
- Jewelcor has announced its 20th store for the suburbs.

[2] "The Suburban Bug Bites Cleveland Catalogers," *Discount Store News*, Vol. 12, No. 16 (July 30, 1973), p. 31.

FIGURE 12 Exterior of the new Best prototype, which has a solo suburban location.

55

FIGURE 13 Exterior of a solo, suburban MacDonald showroom.

- Granjewel is also suburban.
- Basco is booming in the suburbs along with Boardman, Century, and H. B. Davis. Grand Distributors, Naum, Value House, Sutton Place, Summit (with 20 new ones planned for 1973), Louis Schaffer, Sam Solomon. . . .

And we have said nothing about the potential location of possibly hundreds of small independents in any and every town, U.S.A., who have the various *franchising* possibilities open to them.

In any case for most cases—SUBURBAN IS THE SITE.

5

Variations on a Theme

A reason for the new DCS. Its relationship to
the catalog, the catalog counter in Sears, Penney's,
Ward's, and others.

Although approximately 90 percent of sales are
made at the showroom, the DCS gives other options to
its customers. For example, catalogs contain order blanks
that can be sent by mail. In addition, the customer may
pick up her phone and order items that can be picked
up at the will-call in the store. There are other variations
offered by discount stores and supermarkets that have
showrooms on the premises. Let us examine the various
methods available for the DCS customer and relate these

MACDONALD SALES CENTER
10400 Reading Road at Glendale-Milford Road
Evendale, Ohio 45241

NO ENVELOPE NECESSARY
JUST FOLD, SEAL AND MAIL
CHECKS OR MONEY ORDERS MAY BE SAFELY ENCLOSED

TO DETACH TEAR ON PERFORATION

BILL TO

Name _____

Address _____

City _____ State _____ ZIP CODE

Attention of: _____ Phone No. _____

(Do not fill in below unless different from above address)

SHIP TO

Name _____

Address _____

City _____ State _____ ZIP CODE

Attention of: _____

MOVED SINCE LAST ORDER? Write Old Address

Address _____

City _____ State _____ ZIP CODE

DATE _____

MINIMUM ORDER $10
($1 service charge on any
order below this amount)

☐ Check or Money Order Enclosed

Amount: $ . . . .

☐ CHARGE: Open account terms extended
to buyers with satisfactory trade or bank
references. Our terms are net.

Charge by mail with these credit cards:
☐ BankAmericard
☐ Master Charge*

PLEASE FILL IN YOUR CARD NUMBER
AND EXPIRATION DATE ON YOUR
CREDIT CARD, AND SIGNATURE

(Orders not valid unless signed & dated)

Card Number

Signature

Expiration Date

CATALOG Page No.	CATALOG NUMBER	QUANTITY	DESCRIPTION Specify size, color, finish, etc.	SIZE COLOR/FINISH	PRICE EACH	TOTAL AMOUNT

HOW TO ORDER BY MAIL

1. Select the merchandise of your choice.
2. Fill in each line of this order form furnishing catalog page number, stock number of item, quantity, description, size, color or finish, unit price and total amount.
3. Estimate shipping charges from tables on opposite side of form.
4. Enclose remittance, fold and seal order blank where indicated and affix First Class Postage.

1974   PRICES SUBJECT TO CHANGE WITHOUT NOTICE

TOTAL FOR MERCHANDISE	
STATE SALES TAX (IF Applicable)	
TOTAL FOR POSTAGE & INSURANCE	
GRAND TOTAL THIS ORDER	

TO DETACH TEAR ON PERFORATION

FIGURE 14 MacDonald mail order form, which comes in the catalog. Includes directions for use and, on the other side, a postal rate chart.

PLEASE READ CAREFULLY:

1. PLEASE USE DARK PEN, PRINT CLEARLY
2. OPEN ACCOUNTS ONLY TO WELL RATED FIRMS IN D & B.
3. WRITE ANY NOTES OR QUESTIONS ON OTHER SHEET OF PAPER—INCLUDE YOUR NAME AND ADDRESS.
4. PLEASE FILL OUT ORDER BLANK COMPLETELY.
5. ALL MERCHANDISE IS F.O.B. RICHMOND EXCEPT WHERE NOTED. NO C.O.D.—SEND CHECK OR MONEY ORDER WITH ORDER.
6. THIS IS YOUR SHIPPING LABEL — IT MUST BE COMPLETED CLEARLY.

SEND CHECK WITH ORDERS— UNLESS CREDIT HAS BEEN ESTABLISHED

X _____Title.

If this order is to be charged, official signature is required. Account number

FROM
BEST PRODUCTS CO., INC.
4909-13 W. MARSHALL ST.
Richmond, Va. 23230

TO:
Name_____
Attention_____
Address_____
City & State_____ Zip____

CUSTOMER FILL IN

(PRINT CLEARLY)   SOLD TO   FILL IN ONLY IF TO BE SHIPPED TO DIFFERENT ADDRESS

Name_____   SHIP TO   (PRINT CLEARLY)
Attention_____   Name_____
Address_____   Address_____
City & State_____Zip____   City & State_____Zip____

BO = Back order—will be shipped shortly.
DS = Being shipped from factory.
━━ = Lined through items have been or are being shipped separately.
NA = Not available (item is out and will not be reinstated.)
SUB = Similar item substituted.

Quantity, when circled, ⭕ has been shipped.

| BO | DS | NA | SUB |

IF ITEM ORDERED IS OUT OF STOCK, WE WILL SUBSTITUTE A SIMILAR UNIT OF LIKE QUALITY AND PRICE UNLESS ADVISED OTHERWISE

NO ☐

CASH WITH ORDER: If you enclose a check or money order, state the amount sent in this space. Do not send stamps. No C.O.D.'s. $

NOTE: We accept no responsibility for loss or breakage on parcel post shipments unless claims are made within FIVE (5) days of shipment.
On Freight Shipments: The freight company is responsible for loss or damage. Insist on a notation of loss or damage across the face of the freight bill otherwise no claim can be enforced against the freight company.

Please specify page number and catalog number for each item ordered. When stating "quantity" please conform to our unit packaging. Example: if our catalog says "set of 3." order 1 (not 3). If goods are quoted "per doz." order 1 (not 12).

QTY. ORDERED	PAGE NO.	CATALOG NO.	DESCRIPTION (include size, color, etc.)	CODED PRICE	TOTALS
PLEASE USE SEPARATE ORDER BLANK FOR TOYS AND WHEEL GOODS					

DATE	PICKER	PACKER	NO. OF CARTONS
POSTAGE			

MODEL CHANGES
Whenever model changes occur on any item in our Catalog, we will automatically send you the latest model at positive savings.

NEW OPEN ACCOUNT
If new open account desired, include on separate sheet at least two business references and your bank.
Check Here ☐

TOTAL MERCHANDISE	→	
SALES TAX IF EXEMPT, SIGN BELOW	→	
ADD 6% TO APPLY ON DELIVERY CHARGES	→	
50¢ SERVICE CHARGE ON ORDERS LESS THAN $10.00	→	
TOTAL AMOUNT ENCLOSED	→	

COST AND PRICE POLICY: Your coded costs in our Catalog are maintained at the lowest possible level. We invite comparison.
When manufacturers lower our costs during the life of our Catalog, the saving will be passed along to you. When manufacturers increase our cost, we will maintain your lower cost until our stock is depleted. Consequently, all of our customer costs contained in our Catalog are subject to change without notice

SALES TAX EXEMPTION
The undersigned is exempt from Va. and local (if applicable) sales tax.
Signature
Va. Exempt Tax No.
HOW WE SHIP—Orders will be shipped by Parcel Post, United Parcel, Express or Truck—To assure Fast, Safe Delivery. If you require Special Routing of your order please indicate here.
Refunds on over-payments of postage or on merchandise ordered are promptly made.
When we ship your order, you will get a copy of your order blank. Should it be necessary to write, please return order blank with all correspondence.

No Envelope Necessary
JUST FOLD, SEAL AND MAIL
Check or money order, may be safely enclosed

DO NOT WRITE IN SHADED AREAS

FIGURE 14 (Contd.) The Best mail order form. Best puts the rate information on the order form side, and a terms explanation and promotional statement on the back. Both forms fold into a self-sealing envelope.

to possible improvements in the system. Also, a study of
some methods used by the established mail order houses
can give us some insight to possible future developments
in the DCS formula.

I see it—I like it—I want it. The early pioneers in the
self-service food stores who advertised, "desirable merchandise, openly displayed and readily accessible," knew
the value of the possession emotion. This feeling of I WANT
IT and I want it now may be on the wane somewhat.
However, it is long, long from dead. Many of us feel that
we are too materialistic and have thoughts that the next
generation will put fewer dollar signs in the value $y$tem$.
We may be dreaming. In any case, the catalog systems—
no matter how the variation on this theme is arranged—
have the drawback that the customer cannot seemingly
possess the merchandise as readily as in other formulas.

Montgomery Ward is known as the oldest mail order
house in the United States, although Sears may be more
famous to more people as the developer of this retail
distribution formula. Montgomery Ward also *started in
Chicago*. As a central distribution point, Chicago remains
important.

Montgomery Ward's new stores and computerized
effort to have the right merchandise at the right place at
the right time at the right price includes catalog selling
for this company's Century 2. Management seems to be
concerned with the planning and control procedures related to the task and opportunities connected with having
a balanced assortment of merchandise and services to
meet expected and anticipated customer demands. Catalog stores and catalog agencies could develop into catalog
showrooms or indeed discount catalog showrooms. Here

are some highlights of Ward's,[1] which indicate that this company is continually modernizing and the next step may be the DCS.

- 1872—Montgomery Ward, a salesman at Marshall Field, started the business in Chicago in one room with a catalog of one page.
- 1926—Opening of the first store.
- 1931—610 stores in operation.
- 1968—Marcor was formed through the 1968 combination of Montgomery Ward and Container Corporation of America, the largest domestic producer of paperboard packaging.

Retail Stores

- Number   500
- Selling Space   25,000,000 sq. ft.
- Volume   74 percent of Montgomery Ward sales

Catalog Merchandise

- Catalog Stores   700
- Catalog Agencies [2]   1,000
- Sales $600,000,000
- Volume   26 percent of Montgomery Ward sales

[1] All information on Ward's taken from the annual reports of Montgomery Ward and Marcor, and from interviews with Ward Management.

[2] Agents for Montgomery Ward are located in small towns or suburban areas where a company-owned operation may not be worthwhile. An agent could be a housewife or a small retail store. These agents share profits with Montgomery Ward.

- Thirteen annual books including 2 majors and 11 seasonals
- Telephone buying represents 70 percent of sales

Catalog Sales Agencies

- Started in 1966
- An agent can do a $200,000 to $300,000 business in a town of 8,000 to 15,000 population
- Volume   21 percent of catalog sales last year

Montgomery Ward Strategy

- Growth through a double-track new-store program
- Close old stores (which are outdated due to size or population shifts)
- Organization and capture of new markets
- Higher fashion image
- Development of food service
- Opening of new catalog agency
- Implementation of integrated systems
- Personnel development

Ward Organization

- Five regions, which are profit centers for 22 metropolitan districts

Ward Personnel Policy

- Find, develop, and train people to implement the expansion plan
- Retail Management Training Program:
    —12 training programs or units

—Each consists of three activities:
merchandising
operating
managing

—Two store sponsors

—Activities are broken down into companies and tasks

- 1,000 recruits annually for the next several years, 85 percent of them from universities

Credit System

- 51 percent of total sales

Department Stores

- Anchor shopping centers in large, one-store markets and in metropolitan districts where several stores operate under a common advertising umbrella—22 metropolitan districts.
- Size of sales area can range from 70,000 square feet to 160,000 square feet with new prototypes totaling up to 235,000 square feet overall.
- Sell/nonsell ratio currently averaging about 55/45, but new prototypes aiming for 68/32.
- Complete in-store administration, accounting, and merchandising functions may be provided by metropolitan district.
- No self-service.

Three-G Store Characteristics [3]

- Minimal in-store administrative facilities; ac-

[3] Three-G is the new wholly-owned division—third generation —of Montgomery Ward. They are the latest prototype Ward store.

counting and merchandising services provided
centrally for all self-service stores.

- Small-ticket items self-service; big-ticket departments fully staffed for customer assistance; automated POS (point-of-sale) terminals.
- Located in smaller metropolitan markets.
- Use pre-fab construction techniques, with pre-cast, pre-stressed concrete panels and structural components manufactured off site.
- Sell/nonsell space ratio 70/30 accomplished by reduced back room requirements.
- Three standard sizes: 42,000 square feet, 65,000 square feet, and 120,000 square feet of sales area.

Description of a 65,000 Square Foot Three-G-Store

- 150 people
- 60 percent part time
- 40,000 items
- Open 72 hours a week
- 42 departments

Automatic Reordering System

- Point-of-sale data capture
- Daily communication with data processing center
- Automatic processing of new orders
- Generate monthly reports

Plans for the Future

- Agencies   1,500 units by 1975
- Catalog Sales $700 million by 1975

- Selling Space   35 million square feet by 1980
- Sales $3.8 billion by 1980

With this type of expansion for the agencies and catalog sales, it is no wonder that the DCS has some limits on the horizon. Some drawbacks are:

- No expertise in jewelry
- No salespeople knowhow
- Lack of fashion items
- Not one-stop shopping
- Competition from established retail formulas

The *discount* catalog showroom has not yet developed any private labels. In a way, Sears, Ward, and Penney private-label merchandise is nationally branded because of the size and coverage of these companies. The Sears brands have sold in the millions of millions of dollars over the years. Most consumers know the brand names of these large companies and treat them as national brands—comparing prices and quality. These giants can easily open discount operations of the showroom type because customers would believe in the product and have prices to compare.

Sears has the benefit of international feedback. The company can also expand with few formula limitations. For example, the company is now operating in Mexico, Colombia, Brazil, Spain, Belgium, and other countries—such as Japan—are being added to the list continuously. It has been said that the DCS formula has limitations in the United States. Sears, however, can develop this formula—or any formula—with the thought that the whole world is its market. With sales in the reaches of $12 billion, the company can afford developmental and training costs.[4] The Sears breakdown is something like the following, with changes occurring fast:

- 300 department stores
- 400 general merchandise stores
- 200 hard-line stores
- 20 catalog distribution centers
- 2,500 catalog, retail, and telephone sales offices and independent "catalog merchants"

Fifty years ago, Sears was just entering the retail market and the international market. At that time, sales were $200 million—net profits were approaching $15 million and the Employees Profit Sharing Fund was worth over $10 million. It is worth mentioning that Sears has stated in annual reports that employees who share the profits of a business have incentives that will make the enterprise prosper. Today, the Employees Profit Sharing Fund is worth almost $3 billion—the gross national product of a few countries.

Penney is another great name and store and story that should be mentioned briefly here.[5] This Main Street Merchant could also change the development of the DCS. I feel it is very important for anyone interested in the DCS business to take a look at the Sears, Wards, and Penneys in his area. Find out the plans of this competition. I want to underline this competition by showing the development of the J. C. Penney company.

[4] All information about Sears in this section is taken from Sears' annual reports.
[5] All information on Penney taken from its annual reports.

Penney is also a multinational company. Again, I mention this to highlight the fact that developmental costs can be shared in a widespread area over various lines of business. This is a $5 billion company with operations in the United States, Belgium, Italy, and expanding. The company has:

- Department stores
- Soft goods, clothing operations
- TREASURY discount department stores
- THRIFT drug stores
- Supermarkets
- Plus its mail order business

The mail order business is less than ten years old. It was not until 1971 that Penney revealed that this division made a profit. I mention this to point out that this large company is not willing to merely sit around and develop its traditions. It was also not very long ago that James Cash Penney's stores did not sell for anything but cash. Now, credit comprises about one third of the company's total sales.

It could be argued that with all this going on, it is probable that Penney would *not* open catalog stores because it wanted to develop further its present operations. This should have been the case before this giant ventured into other activities—such as food—but this is not so. The company management is provided with speedy, accurate information regarding areas of profitability, and it seems that the company is not in the retailing business but the money-making business.

A particular variation on the theme of catalog selling has been developed by Penney. The company has some

1,200 catalog sales centers. Most of these are connected with their retail operations. In some small stores, the "catalog sales center" is merely a telephone and a catalog. The telephone is connected with an "order taker, sales associate" located in the store or somewhere in the vicinity. The idea is that if you cannot find it in the store, please order it from the catalog desk.

DCS's ARE INTERESTED IN REDUCING MERCHANDISE AS-SORTMENT AND THE INVESTMENT IN INVENTORY. The inventory asset seems to continuously grow as the computer comes up with new colors, new combinations of styles, and new fabric formulas. On the other hand, customer service keeps the customer coming back because this individualizes a particular retail unit. The catalog can help give the assortment without having the cash tied up in merchandise either in the store or in the back room. Of course, it must be available somewhere, and anyone with two or more stores knows that the game of "back and forth" to get rid of markdowns is a costly one.

The next step for stores such as Sears, Penney, Ward, or any small or large operation is to have a catalog show-room with all the cost-saving devices already tested in the typical discount catalog showroom—in addition to the catalog. This will be the best of both worlds. One-stop shopping is always appealing, and prices can be the lowest in town by utilizing the automation and mechanization of the discount catalog formula. It will be interesting to see how the DCS will affect the traditional catalog sales of Sears, Penney, Spiegel, and the others who have great reputations in catalog selling. The difference between the two is that the customer comes into the discount catalog showroom to see the merchandise before the final decision to purchase the item is made. Through mail order, the customer does not have the opportunity to view the merchandise until it arrives in the mail.

Another advantage of the DCS over the traditional mail-order formula is the possibility of impulse sales. When the customer comes into the DCS, she almost always has made a decision from first looking at specifications in the catalog. But when she is there, she is tempted by the "self-service" items (those that are readily available—they do not have to be brought from the back room but can be carried to the checkout just as in the regular discount department store) or she is tempted to fill in another item on the order blank along with the item she came to buy. Many DCS operators are now shifting to "not-in-catalog" merchandise. This not only increases impulse sales, it also offers merchandise without the embarrassment of out of stocks. If it is not in the catalog, the customer will not be *planning* to buy it, and so will not be disappointed by an out-of-stock situation. Also, not-in-catalog merchandise assortments afford individual showrooms a chance to cater to their locale's specific merchandising needs, a chance that is not necessarily provided by a catalog coordinator's nationally sold book. Of course strictly mail-order retailers cannot take advantage of this opportunity.

Sears, Ward, and others may not be interested in joining the DCS boom because their own stores may suffer. On the other hand, the showroom could complement their other system. Let us wait and see.

Of course, established retailers do not *have* to join the parade. However, actions and reactions are already occurring, and other ventures are taking the time of Sears and Ward. For example, Sears is now selling in Japan from a Sears catalog on display at the Seibu department stores.

6

The Biggies Enter

As the discount catalog showroom proves its worth, more and more established firms have entered this field. Some of the well-known retailing giants that have entered this type of selling include Grant, May Department Stores, and Giant Food. Each has added a new dimension to the applied techniques of the discount catalog showroom formula. The following pages give some of the innovations by the Biggies who have tried their own hand.

Special thanks go to the management and employees of the discount catalog showrooms who very kindly answered questions and showed me their operations. No special secrets of sales, net profits, expense figures, and so on will be told here. However, much is to be learned directly from the people on the firing line. Most of the interviews were granted in the Dayton-Cincinnati; Washington, D.C.-Richmond; and New York areas. All took place during the Christmas season of 1972 and early to mid-1973. The replies are composite answers and are not attributed to any one manager or DCS operation.

QUESTION: How important is price in the discount catalog showroom?

ANSWER: It is the most important factor in bringing customers to the store. Other factors include convenient locations with free parking, desirable merchandise, long store hours, as well as something new. The catalog showroom is something new, and the housewife likes to shop in someplace new and different.

QUESTION: Are diamond rings your number-one item?

ANSWER: We don't have that information available, but I can say that jewelry is number one with us. Here, the traditional stores have a few sales but prices are too high. As a matter of fact, we could say that we have most of the other items just so that people will come in here to buy diamond rings and other fine gold and silver items. Of course, the prices are right. People hesitate to just come in and look at diamond rings, but they always look at them after buying a cheaper item. [Author's note: This threshold resistance idea is extremely important and needs to be stressed here. Most discount showroom retailers fully intend to make the customer feel at home in the jewelry areas even when the fixtures and setting are highly luxurious. There is no doubt that few people walk in off the street to look at expensive jewelry items unless there is a very serious intention to buy at that particular store. Even in this day and age, people are still intimidated by store salespeople in this category.] (The author was told that customers bought diamond rings in every case—as well as all merchandise—in catalog showrooms because of low prices. In a few cases, store management said that customers also came because of store location but that price was more important.)

QUESTION: Are returns very high?

ANSWER: No. Returns run less than 1 percent because the customer sees the item in the catalog and in the showroom. Very few—probably less than 5 percent —actually look at the item in the store. Most will look at the carton to see if the proper color is listed. Returns run higher after Christmas because of gifts. However, most people buy gifts that they know are wanted. In most cases, our customers come in with a catalog checked off and just fill in the information from the catalog. At Christmas time or Mother's Day, the housewife might check off several items, and the husband or children come in and look at a selection. That gives them a choice, and they buy one or two of the items. Actually we have thought of promoting the fact that now gift giving will be easier because the person receiving the gift can make several actual selections and then expect to get one of those listed. Of course, there is some stigma about the price, but I think most people know how much gifts that they get cost anyway. We get a few returns due to damage, but I think most of the people damage them and bring them back afterward. Manufacturers are increasingly unwilling to take back some of these items but do a fine job in servicing. Our company does not do any servicing, but we have very good relations with the local service organization of these nationally branded items—especially appliances. Because we do not have fashion items (we promoted shirts and ties in boxes all wrapped up at Christmas time and had them at the checkout on a self-service basis at a very good price—both manufacturer and retail listed—and we did very well. Some of these came back, the housewife saying that the size or color was not acceptable. However, we do not have fashion for this reason. Too many returns, and then people want advice and expect to try on the merchandise. Now we have really trained people in the jewelry department but otherwise we have no trained people), we can have a minimum number of people on the sales-floor at slow periods. We don't have to worry about answering questions. The catalog does that.

QUESTION: What about pilferage and your overall shrink?

ANSWER: The customer and employee thefts are very low compared to a retail store's 3 to 4 percent (truthful figure) of a store in this type of merchandise. Our figure is really about 1 percent, and this includes everything. And of course we do not have special sales, which sometimes hide real losses. We do not have any markdowns.

QUESTION: Your order form has six lines. Is this enough? Does the customer use more than one? What are the various parts used for? Is it inventory control? And one further item—is it necessary to show the example to guide the customer since it takes up one complete line?

ANSWER: We have tested up to ten lines. We use one now

for the example, which is very important, especially
for new customers and to get the information done
properly. Yes, at Christmas time the customers used
more than one form. We tried a long 8½ by 11 inch
form or just a bit smaller but it was too cumbersome.
The customers like this half-sheet form with the six
lines. Most of our orders, except for jewelry, are for
two items. Many are for one, but sometime we have
six merchandise items on an order, sometimes more.
Usually we have no more than four. The average sale
is about $21.00. This includes jewelry. We haven't
available complete information on this. We don't
have all of our five checkouts going (three at the
pay-point and two at the jewelry counter) at one
time. Yes, the form is for inventory control. One
part of the form goes with the customer, one with
the checkout, one for notations (stockholds or stockouts) and one for our computer system in the basement. Stockhold is connected with will-call. About
85 percent of the merchandise comes under a complete electronic data processing (EDP) control system. For example, the order form filled in by the
customer goes to the warehouse EDP keypunch operator. This form keeps the computer updated regarding items sold and level of stock. Some stores use
only a three-part order form, and I guess that one
copy goes to the customer with the merchandise, one
to the EDP system, and one for emergency use such
as stockouts. We have as many as 8 girls in will-call
during peak periods. We have a special room with
telephones and then the customers come to the will-
call desk and get the merchandise and pay at the
same time. We have a mail order, too, but that goes
to our main office, and we charge for mailing and,

for small items, for handling. We are testing health and beauty aids and maybe more candy to be added to our rack-jobber items such as softgoods now. For these, we will not have a ticket for inventory. The rack jobber takes care of the inventory control because we do not have the staff. Our staff is 10 full-time and 60 part-time who work from 10 to 30 hours in 10-hour time frames, depending upon the time of year. We usually find that we have 95 percent of the items on hand at all times due to our inventory control system. We have visual checks all the time, too. When we do not have an item, we try to get the customer to switch, but that is difficult because the staff is not trained to do so although we have some training films and discussions on this planned even for the part-timers.

QUESTION: Do you have a *consumers' panel?*

ANSWER: You mean like some stores get housewives together once a month or so for a free coffee to exchange ideas and complain? No, we don't, but I think it is a good idea. What we do have is a form asking for suggestions, asking for ideas and other things like what type of items would they like in our next catalog. The card is postage paid and addressed to the head of the company. We get a few of these. The return is not high, but at first we passed them out at the store openings and got back several hundred. Now it is only a few a week. But customers like to see them there. I think some of the people take them but don't fill them out or send them in. We have them located at our service counters and our order tables.

Dear Customer,

Please check the appropriate boxes.

	YES	NO
1. DID YOU FIND WHAT YOU WERE LOOKING FOR?	☐	☐
2. HAD YOU SELECTED AN ITEM FROM OUR CATALOG BEFORE YOU CAME INTO OUR SHOWROOM?	☐	☐
3. DID YOU LOOK AT NON-CATALOG ITEMS AFTER YOU CAME?	☐	☐
4. DID YOU NOTICE OUR "TRU-SPECIALS"?	☐	☐
5. WHAT OTHER TYPES OF MERCHANDISE WOULD YOU LIKE BEST PRODUCTS TO HANDLE?	☐	☐

Additional Comments and Suggestions _____

_____

_____

_____

_____

_____

_____

_____

If you wish,

include your name and address for acknowledgement of your confidential comments.

Name_____
(PLEASE PRINT)

Street_____

City _____ State _____ Zip_____

	YES	NO
DO YOU RECEIVE A BEST PRODUCTS CATALOG?	☐	☐
IF NOT, SHALL WE PUT YOU ON OUR PERMANENT MAILING LIST? (SEND $1.00 TO RECEIVE **ALL** FUTURE CATALOGS.)	☐	☐

As a satisfied customer, you are our greatest asset, and it is my earnest desire that we please you. If you experience something that is good or bad, or feel that there is room for improvement, I would appreciate hearing about it.

Thank you.   *S. Lewis*
                                   President

Moisten at top to seal — Please drop in slot or mail — No postage needed.

FIGURE 15 Best's customer questionnaire, which asks for comments and suggestions in addition to the questions at the top of the form. This folds into a self-envelope.

QUESTION: I notice you seem to feature four self-service items: men's underwear, greeting cards and related party items, candles and wrapping paper. Have you tested these?

ANSWER: We keep shifting these around. However, I think we will stay with and even expand gift wrappings. Many of our items are for gifts, and people don't mind paying extra for self-tied bows and very good paper. Of course, it is cheaper than conventional stores and just a bit less or very competitive with hard-hitting discounters. A check showed that somewhere around 30 to 35 percent is bought for gifts. Much of our business is done at Christmas season, and I guess gifts would be a much higher percentage at that time. We haven't done a survey. (Author's note: the supplement to *Discount Store News*, April 23, 1973, entitled, "Untapped Profits in Luggage" on page S9 has some interesting statistics regarding luggage sold in catalog showrooms. For example, it is mentioned that Lebhar-Friedman Research talked to several hundred catalog showroom customers. Here it is shown that luggage was purchased for gift-giving purposes for 35 percent of those interviewed. An interesting part of this research showed that of these customers:

- 52 percent would like good displays in shopping for luggage
- 30 percent wanted quality products
- 22 percent said selection counted
- 18 percent included guarantee as important)

QUESTION: Will you expand store hours?

ANSWER: No—we are "rationalizing" them now. I mean we are trying to decide which hours are the most profitable. We will open more during busy seasons and close more in off times I think. Right now, we are still trying to get a history of sales and profitable item selling such as jewelry. Most of the time, we will close on Sundays and be open from 10 to 6, except maybe Fridays or Thusdays until 9. Right now, those are our hours. At Christmas, we are open Sunday noon to 6 and every night until 10. Next year, we might stay open until 11 P.M. or so. (Author's note: One company in Ohio last November secured a diamond worth $250,000 for show and possible sale. This was a cocktail type of showing with Pinkerton guards in white goves, cars being parked, long gowns, and so on. In addition, the jewelry department was open for purchases but the rest of the store was closed. These "after hours" sales could become a sales technique as is done now by furniture and department stores.)

QUESTION: Why are you so upgraded in your fixturing and carpeting?

ANSWER: Here in the Washington (D.C.) area, most of the stores have upgraded, and even those with discount images have added expensive fixtures. We are carpeted because it is hoped that this will cut down display damage and also it is expected that the cleaning and the maintenance will be easier. Also, we want the people to think of us as a discounter for expensive items—not just another discounter. We want them to buy jewelry, and that is why we have the jewelry counter just as they enter the store from the other part of our business.

QUESTION: Do you have trouble in getting merchandise from manufacturers?

ANSWER: We have been in business for a long time as distributors, and we have very good relations with manufacturers. They will supply the traditional lines that we have carried for the trade for a long time. We are listed still as distributors, and that is why we have customers fill in a card with the companies they work for who are usually our customers. We are still distributors for incentive awards, business gifts, and employee gifts as well as being open to "selected public."

QUESTION: How are you organized? What are your major departments?

ANSWER: I am the General Manager plus I have a co-manager or assistant manager. We have an Operations Manager who has a co-manager, and it is the same for the warehouse manager. We have area managers and each has an assistant or co-manager in sporting goods, toys, jewelry, and a general merchandise area manager. The Operations Manager is in charge of cashiering, the greeters, the service desk, the maintenance, the payroll, the store hours adjustment. Usually the store is open 10 to 10 plus noon to 6 on Sunday, but we have adjustments. He is also responsible for advertisement, which is usually 2 percent of sales. The store here is planned to do about $10 million per year. The co-manager of operations spends his time in receiving and the back room and is really the manager back there. Two full-time boys are back there, but we are having a promotion soon, and that is why we have the two extras. I have been working back here, too, because we have merchandise piled all over the place for this promotion. Our back room is twice as large, exactly, as the showroom area. That includes the sporting goods and toys areas, which have their own separate checkouts. Right now we have a cash register at the camera section with films in back because of pilferage.

QUESTION: Do you get many mail orders?

ANSWER: Here in the East, we have some areas that are just remote enough that we get an order consistently from the same family. However, our mail order is a very small part of the business. We have thought of dropping it because we want the customers to make impulse buys in our silver, sporting goods, jewelry, and so on, where we get good markups. There is some competition from European mail order, too. *Quelle* has an office here in West New York, New Jersey, and they have a big promotion going on their Big Lift delivery by air. This Quelle system Big Lift lets the customer get UPS (United Parcel Service) or air mail without losing the money involved in the recent currency devaluation. Quelle is the biggest mail order house in Europe with headquarters in Germany. We don't try to compete with them but really try to get the customer in the store.

QUESTION: Do you own, maintain, and so on, your building?

ANSWER: The company has a buy-build-lease-back arrangement. We also have an outside cleaning service as well as outsiders for the parking lot and refuse disposal. We used consultants for the building, and all our new ones are alike.

QUESTION: Do you see your type of business becoming a regular retail store?

ANSWER: No. We don't want to become just another retailer with all the competition. We also do not want to compete in all the advertising expense, service and wages costs, promotions, delivery, and all that. Our average is a low 22 percent, and most stores can't compete with this, so I think customers will come here with our system to get these low prices. There are about 1,500 catalog showrooms now, and by 1975 there is supposed to be about 2,500 or so. Sales for our group is about $1.500 billion now, and this is supposed to be about $5 billion by 1975. Our big advantages are also other areas of low overhead, no shrink problem, and our customers like the at-home shopping or pre-shopping.

QUESTION: You are a manager of a very large mail order house branch store in the suburbs. There are two discount catalog showrooms not too far away. Are you losing sales to them?

ANSWER: Our sales are increasing over past years but we could lose sales in the future. I know the so-called mail order houses are thinking about catalog showrooms, too. Of course, we have had catalog selling for many years. In a sense, we also have these types of stores. For example, we have places where the customer can go and order and come back very soon (sometime the next couple of days) and pick up the merchandise. I don't think the customer wants to have everything right away anyway. Customers like delivery, too. Catalog stores do not have low-price points and our stores and catalog do. We also have the advantage of personal selling in both the catalog and the store. For catalog selling, usually the orders are called in or the people come to the store. Of course, we can't upgrade or suggest-sell by mail, but we can by telephone and by counter mail orders. The number of people who come back to the same person or ask for the same person by telephone when placing an order is surprising.

QUESTION: You have two stores open now. What about the Biggies? Do you think larger organizations will come in and take your business later on—business that will be profitable, such as jewelry?

ANSWER: No. So far, there are several big companies in the business—I guess most of them are testing and thinking. We hear rumors all the time. May Department Stores is the only one who has made really big announcements and commitments it seems to me. Besides, we have buying services and coordinators who can buy as cheap, or maybe cheaper, than the big companies. We get help with the catalog, buying, advice, and many special deals and closeouts. Our group supplies over 10,000 outlets and has continuous contact with almost 500 big manufacturers.

QUESTION: What about the future?

ANSWER: I think we will grow and grow and put many stores out of business.

7

The Establishment Reacts

The Establishment Reacts. While some large companies (even food-oriented companies such as Giant Food of Washington, D.C.) join 'em, others are fighting. Additional interviews and facts and figures on companies such as Service Merchandise and Jewelcor.

THE MISSION OF MERCHANDISING. The objective of distribution is to have the right merchandise at the right place at the right time at the right price. There is also the *concept of materiality* (actual dollars involved rather than percentage figures). You can't put percentages in the bank—nor do we need to worry about small penny losses, which permits us to make a few mistakes in some areas. For example, in retailing, we can make a few errors in ordering or in records, and the customer will keep patronizing our stores. We cannot make any errors in cash, however, unless—with most people it seems—we give the customer *too much* change. However, there is a change in standards of living, education levels, housewives working, and leisure time.

Consequently, it seems that the customer wants not only the right merchandise but the lowest possible price. It means not only at the right place (convenient to the customer's house) but on hand for take-home. So, catalog showrooms grow in number because the formula permits the customer to get the lowest price and yet the merchandise is readily available. Let us look at the growth of some of the public companies who have published annual reports and who have granted interviews.

JEWELCOR INCORPORATED AND SUBSIDIARIES. Mr. Seymour Holtzman, President of Jewelcor, has said that catalog showrooms usually do not produce a profit during the first calendar quarter of the year. His company has had some very fine results. Jewelcor had only one catalog showroom when sales were at $3.5 million plus. With eight in operation, sales pushed toward the $8 million mark with profits going from near the $400,000 point to near the $600,000 figure. This was before taxes. Some recent openings include:

- Jacksonville, Florida: 25,000 sq. ft., opened 1972
- Wilkes-Barre, Pennsylvania: 60,000 sq. ft., opened fall 1973
- Harrisburg, Pennsylvania, Allentown, Pa.: both 25,000 sq. ft., opened 1972

- Indianapolis, Indiana: 25,000 sq. ft., opened spring 1973

Jewelcor has been very busy. Starting in 1971, the company offered common stock to the public; acquired a catalog showroom in June in Ft. Lauderdale, Florida; acquired a watch distributor; and completed a printing plant. Other catalog showrooms opened in Lancaster (Vanity Fair) and Indianapolis (Golden Company showroom). Other acquisitions included:

- National Wholesale Distributors (Mobile, Alabama showroom)
- National Jewelers and Distributors (Pensacola, Florida showroom)

Jewelcor has three divisions:

- Catalog showrooms and catalog publication (it is becoming a very large coordinator)
- Precious jewelry manufacturing and distribution
- Commercial printing and related graphic arts activities

Company sales have gone from $3.6 million in 1967 to almost $40 million in 1973. Net profits are equally impressive. The Jewelcor organization is as follows:

- The Jewelry division manufactures and sells to the catalog division
- The Graphic Arts Division prints for the catalog division

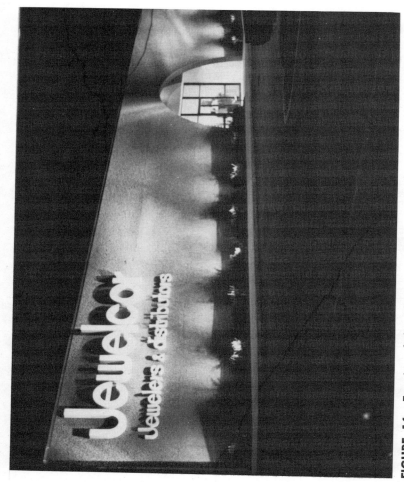

FIGURE 16 Exterior of the Allentown, Pennsylvania, Jewelcor showroom. Courtesy of *Discount Store News.*

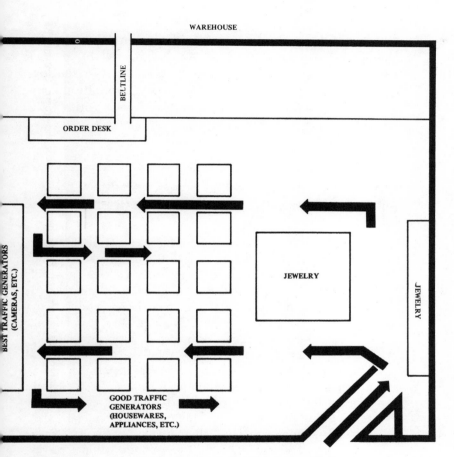

FIGURE 17 Typical Jewelcor layout, which has a 45-degree angle for entrance and immediate exposure to jewelry counters. This layout was designed to pull customers through entire showroom. Courtesy of *Discount Store News*.

- The several associated companies prepare catalogs

In addition, the various subsidiary companies sell to
chains and department stores. Also, some sell to several
wholesalers as well as to catalog showrooms—including
those owned and operated by Jewelcor. Corporate offices
are at 1212 Avenue of the Americas, New York, N.Y.
10036.

Page 2 of the Jewelcor 1971 *Annual Report* sum-
maries the catalog showroom business and this company's
philosophy.

The catalog showroom business is a relatively new
and somewhat novel approach to the merchandising and
sale of various goods and items such as jewelry, small
appliances, home electronics and giftwares. As employed
by your Company, a catalog compiled and produced by
our own Srago Associated Catalogs, Inc., containing
jewelry and brand name items listed at prices generally
below those of conventional retailers, is distributed
throughout the various marketing areas serviced by your
company's catalog showroom-warehouses. In the comfort of his home, a buyer can pre-shop the merchandise
he wishes to purchase, and later, at his convenience, visit
the showroom-warehouse where he fills out his own order
slip, pays the cashier, and at a separate counter, picks
up his purchase. The nature and design of our showrooms are such that one of a representative number of
items in the catalog is generally on display supported
by complete back-up inventory in the warehouse portion
of the building. As a result, the national problem of

shoplifting is substantially reduced while costly floor and display space is minimized. In addition, since the customers have pre-shopped their purchases, sales personnel and therefore labor costs are considerably reduced. Taken as a whole, the operation affords consumers a convenient, economic and expeditious means for the satisfaction of many of their shopping needs.

Please note that there is no indication that *one-stop shopping* will be pursued by this company. However, there are the stores of the Giant Food Company in the Washington, D.C. area that are entered from the side of the Giant supermarkets. Furniture and true fashion items are not available, but Giant's approach is moving toward these complete shopping trips. The furniture warehouse might be teamed with the supermarket and the catalog showroom for a new formula in distribution and a real one-stop shopping experience.

THE DISCOUNTING CYCLE. As already mentioned, many, many of our established retailers started as discounters in some form. In addition, many of the self-service, discount department stores (SSDDS) started in 1955 or so by being very strong in one or two divisions and gradually added additional departments. The largest of them all today, K mart, has not incorporated all departments into company operations. By now Kresge's K marts are truly discounting's "establishment," but no word about the discount catalog showroom. The annual report of Kresge indicates that in 1972 some 92 K marts were opened representing 6,478,000 square feet. No doubt that is enough to keep them busy without worrying about adding food or taking on a new line such as the DCS. During 1973, K marts have opened in 100 new locations.

Kresge must also be praised for opening their new international headquarters along with this store expansion.

Of course Kresge could expand its one-stop shopping image by adding a *catalog desk* (maybe even with telephone) as some of the new Penney units have done. The K mart (or Kresge) catalog could be smaller than Penney's or Sears' or Ward's. The limit of *500 pages* seems to be a "rule of maximum" for most catalog showrooms. Kresge might make this decision to keep the conventional DCS away from its good sites. Originally, most DCS's were in areas on the other side of the tracks. Now they are in locations very near K marts in the suburbs. In Dayton, Ohio, on Salem Avenue Best is not very far away from K mart, and it's on the same side of the street. The Best is just across the way from Gold Circle in that location. We could wonder also about catalog selling and a showroom for Gold Circle, the subsidiary of Federated Department Stores. Federated has experience with mail order and catalogs on a very limited scale. Through its furniture and other warehouse stores, there has been some experience gained. My five years working with Federated (an employee in a department store division) tells me that this outstanding organization is willing to try, and their record shows that they do. The executives are not a bashful bunch, and the money keeps rolling in. These boys have suburban experience with only just over 36 percent of the sales coming from downtown units these days.

THE SMALL ESTABLISHMENT. Other traditional, smaller organizations are also experimenting with the DCS formula. Alexander's (of New York City) is seeking its third site for a 1973 opening. Forbes & Wallace—that pillar of downtown Springfield, Massachusetts, is to open its first soon. Elder-Beerman department stores of Dayton, Ohio, will join the DCS crowd. Grand Union seems to be converting 60,000 square feet former Grand Way discounters into discount catalog showrooms. Granjewel (W. T. Grant and Jewelcor) will open in some former W. T. Grant locations. Robert Hall and Super Valu are also joining the DCS movement.

A DRIVE TO SPRINGFIELD, OHIO. Recently a Century DCS (Century Housewares, Inc.) closed on Salem Avenue in Dayton, Ohio. It could be the pressure from the new and bigger Best down the road, or a number of other factors. The location in a small, neighborhood-to-community size shopping center (in a former metropolitan clothing store branch) was not the best, perhaps. We asked the establishment about the closing, and many said the management was not alert enough—although I had shopped the store and found most activity, on the outside only, of course, to be very good. In any case, I learned that a new unit was to open in Springfield—about 30 miles away. This little city has plenty of establishment already there. A beautiful EMAC, just a year old, has large Rikes, Sears, and Penney's among its stores. Just down highway (Interstate) 70 outside Columbus, a new Penney distribution center is springing up. A new Sears center opened last year. Everyone seems to be enjoying a boom in sales (Penney's was up 28 percent) via catalog. Why would the Century close?

Century Housewares has 32 or so discount catalog showrooms. Reports are that it is trying to increase mail orders (from the current reported 1 percent). This could mean fewer showrooms such as the one in Dayton. The story is that the mail customer gets the item at a mere 6 percent above Century's cost. The Springfield drive shows another reason: bigger Century showrooms for the new image. The new Century tries to display one each of every catalog item. This certainly could add to the possible impulse buys. Springfield's unit is over 50,000 square feet. The original unit, opened in 1954, had 28,000 square feet.

OTHER ESTABLISHMENTARIANS. FedMart issued a lively catalog. Clarkins (another Ohio group—a division of Unishops) also has a catalog. Department stores are issuing larger catalogs. Add to this the experiments of Murphy and Zayre, and the DCS movement has many actions and reactions by established stores to dam its flow of expansion somewhat. However, this list of expansion goes on and on.

- Century is selling $40 million and expanding as mentioned
- Best is moving into the 65,000 square footers
- Belscot is expanding in Chicago
- MacDonald is expanding in the Ohio area
- Bell is booming
- Carlson, Ciro, and Cooper are growing
- Gaylord National Corporation, Holda, and Howard Bros. are active
- L. Luria & Son operates in Miami
- Naum Bros. got burning publicity when they took advantage of a fire in a New York City store
- David Weis will fight in Monroeville, Pa.
- Ross Furniture, Sal Solomon, Altman Department Stores, Modern Merchandising of Minneapolis, Minnesota—are going into the DCS business

Some of the above will be located in former discount stores—such as Shoppers Fair or Atlantic or Pathmark or

Town & Country (of Lane Bryant). Others, and I have not mentioned the fine Service Merchandise group, GEX, Zale Corporation, Fashion Showcase (Unity Buying Service), Dahnken East, Esco, and so on, are going into new buildings that have all the features and operating techniques of a discount department store.

GEX—AN ESTABLISHED MEMBERSHIP LEADER. Some companies charge rather high membership fees. Some are small—such as MacDonald's $1.00 lifetime membership. The Unity group charges $6.00 yearly with renewal rates as high as 40 percent. Unity's active membership at the end of last year was over 560,000 compared with some 380,000 twelve months earlier. This leads us to compare catalog showrooms with the membership discount stores. Every sizable U.S. city had one or two of these MDS's, and most have now gone out of business or opened their doors to the non-card-carrying public.

The Fashion Look. A feature of Unity's recent catalog was a 16-page fashion supplement. This could really get reactions from Federated, Allied, and Associated Department stores. We can almost see a catalog unit in all May Department Store branches. The compact unit of 9,300 square feet that May's partner—Consumers Distributing, Ltd.—likes could put some activity into May's conventional stores. Consumers Distributing, Ltd., has almost 100 units in operation and is expected to open 150 with May. Consumers' strategy is to open these small units surrounding a city rather than one or at most two in the city, which seems to be the feeling of Best and others. May may have some feeling against the two-price policy, but most people seem to feel that the potential Federal Trade Commission rulings outlawing catalog price codings will not disrupt the industry. The merchandise mix might, however. Adding fashion items could mean huge stores and servic-

ing. Showrooms such as Service Merchandise Company
units already feature 12,000 different items on display.

SERVICE MERCHANDISE. The annual report shows sales
for this company doubling every couple of years. The last
report also shows net income doubling. Of course, these
companies are now small, and just one or two showrooms
can double the sales figure. Service was selling $16 mil-
lion plus in 1971, $20 million plus in 1972, and so on.
Service is adding four or five new showrooms each year
with the pace accelerating. The 1972 annual report sums
up their system very well.

"The customer makes a selection of merchandise
either from the catalog or from the display shelves and
enters it on the form provided. The customer then turns
in her selection form at the information and order-entry
counter. The clerk at this station reviews the form for
completeness and sends it by pneumatic tube to the warehouse. An employee in the warehouse receives the order.
After checking the huge directory board for location, warehouse personnel quickly pick the merchandise and place
it on the conveyor belt which travels to the customer
pickup station. Personnel here remove the order, mark
the attached order form, and pass two copies to the
cashier, leaving one attached to the merchandise. The
cashier pages the customer by name, validates the order
forms on the cash register and receives payment. One
copy of the form goes to the customer. The customer
presents the form to the checkout station employee who
validates it with the form on the merchandise in the
numbered bin and delivers the order to the customer."

THE SYSTEMS AND THE FINANCING. At the present time,
no pattern of a financial or management information system can be established for discount catalog showrooms.
The established companies—such as May department

stores—have loans available from companies such as Metropolitan Life Insurance ($25 million was borrowed by a
May subsidiary) and banks. The newcomers who do not
have the established lines of credit have gone public
(usually American Exchange) or have borrowed from their
local bank. Some earlier reports showed tremendous return on average shareholders' equity. Modern Merchandising, Inc. (formerly Jetoro, Inc.) in its 1971 report showed
such a return at 41.3 percent.

MODERN MERCHANDISING. Recent reports of this Minneapolis company show 60 percent net income and 90
percent sales increases. No established company has such
results. But, billions of dollars should not be compared
with millions without some detailed explanation. The activities of such companies as Modern Merchandising is
closing this tremendous gap. La Belle's and other MM
divisions, such as Anchor Distributors, have been in business since 1946 and are opening stores in new locations,
too.

HOPE FOR THE LITTLE JEWELER. Tiffany will not go
out of business from competition with the discount catalog
showroom. (Author's opinion.) However, small jewelers
in both downtown and shopping strip or shopping center
locations *have already gone out of business* due to the
DCS competition. I have observed this in Washington,
D.C., New Jersey, and Ohio. The fight of big versus little
is nothing new. The Mom and Pop corner grocer began
to face it in 1916 with the chains and again with the large
supermarkets in the 1930s. Small textile and clothing
stores faced this in the late 1950s fighting against the large
self-service, discount department stores. *Survival has come
by fighting on different grounds. This again must be the
case.* The big store is efficient, but cold and indifferent.
There are no people to greet or serve the customer in the

same highly personal way available to the small store owner or operator. If he will shift to becoming an artist of retailing he can not only stay in business but expand. There are enough customers to go around. Most will pay for that something extra. Usually it is not there, and we, the consuming public, choose self-service rather than "bad" service. Service is the way Tiffany—and other famous service stores, including Neiman-Marcus—has always fought.

Of course, Neiman-Marcus and Tiffany are not independents any more either. But they both continue to do catalog selling. This idea of threshold resistance comes in again. People may be hesitant to visit Tiffany or Neiman's but they will order out of their catalogs. People do like labels. And it is easy to spend our way out of boredom through the catalog, too. It has been said that we work harder and longer to buy goods, which means we have less time to enjoy these goods. In any case, it is always a pleasure to look through the fine catalogs of fine stores— as well as the catalogs of the traditional houses and the new DCS.

SOME ARGUMENTS AGAINST BY THE ESTABLISHMENT. Dayton-Hudson said it was cutting back its research and activities in the catalog showroom operations in order to better use capital in other areas. In July 1972, Dayton-Hudson acquired Sibley Co. and Consolidated Merchandising Corporation, which together had DCS sales of about $5 million. At the same time, Sakowitz in Houston reported that plans were underway to expand its sales via direct mail and catalog from 3 percent of store volume to 10 percent within the next few years. Growth (adding 500,000 to mailing lists) will come from present non-customers.

Through my interviews I found that most large and

small established companies feel that at the present time they are doing well enough so that the threat from discount catalog showrooms is not so great as that from the expanding activities of the conventional discount department store. Some management felt that the DCS would not expand because of inflation in preparing the catalog and in mailing costs. Also, it is difficult to raise prices even though catalogs show somewhere that prices are subject to increases without notice. Other management felt that upgrading would continue to occur and that the DCS would not be able to keep up with it fast enough because of the built-in structuring of the formula. Still more feelings about rent (now 1 percent to 2 percent) may indicate that prices will have to be increased as this and other expenses go up. Other statements went:

"As the number of items must be increased, the handling costs will have to go up. The picking board in the backroom will become so complicated that the time lag will increase and the customer will not wait."

"Stockturns will slow from the three to five to the conventional."

"Pilferage will go up as people will learn how to beat the present controls in the DCS."

"The merchandising in all the DCS's is the same . . . customers will be bored with the same old store type."

"Already they are going out of business or consolidating. Before long, the old rule that 20 percent will do 80 percent of the business will apply, and the growth will slow to the usual 5 to 8 percent."

"The 5 to 8 percent of sales for payroll will go up to conventional rates as services are added."

"Coded prices is being changed by legislation and that will end the DCS."

"We can drop prices below the DCS on loss leaders, and they cannot react because their prices are fixed in the catalog."

"Already discounters are taking over the initiative in showrooms. For example, Holda's of Jackson, Michigan, is teaming up with Rink's, and both will share a common parking lot."

"Manufacturers will no longer be able to sell to catalog showrooms at special prices, lower than to regular retailers, as will be proved in the General Electric Distribution case."

"The DCS is too fad oriented."

"Reducing lines to one or two choices will drive customers away."

"Companies who have money will expand catalog showrooms to get the high return on investment, but when this drops they will stop. For example, May Department Stores has a margin of about 40 percent in their department stores with a net of about 2 percent and a return of 10 percent. Then they tried discount stores (VENTURE), and with a margin of 23 percent or so they got less than 2 percent net after taxes but a return of almost 15 percent. Now they are trying DCS stores to get even higher returns, as the showrooms are not upgraded. Their discount stores got upgraded, and the returns dropped. This will happen in this new industry, too."

A glance at retailing history shows that similar arguments appeared against the new department store, supermarket, and most recently, the discount department store. There is no doubt that when the customer does the work there are savings. Also there is no doubt that a new store attracts. Growth will certainly slow for the discount catalog showroom as it has for the supermarket and the self-service discount department store. But in the meantime, many established retailers will close. Pause for a moment and count the famous department stores that have come to an end within the past 15 years as the SSDDS expanded. And the number of closed small grocery stores reaches into the hundreds of thousands. . . .

8

The Important
Return on Investment Factor

While retailing and distribution in general is having a hard time showing a proper ROI (return on investment), the DCS industry is coming up with 20 percent to 30 percent—or more.

A MILLION AND AN IDIOT EQUALS A MILLION. It has been said that even an idiot can show a net profit in a retail store if he has a million dollars to spend.

Traditionally in retailing, it is the net profits on sales that have determined success. Now, return on investment is becoming more and more important. These are, of course, related, but the difference is great. The question is: "How long do you want to wait to get your money back?" If you are building for your grandchildren or great-grand-children, maybe you are pleased if the store breaks even without any consideration for opportunity costs and return on the capital you have invested—especially if it is extra capital. If not, the DCS is one of the fastest and best ways of securing high ROI's today.

In addition to the subjective considerations of having one's name on the new cathedral of retailing rather than on that old roadside store now that you have joined the country club, there is that serious consideration of inflation, sale, going public, or merging with another company and living on the sale and return of *their* stock.

Certainly, many famous family department stores have joined large national conglomerchants for this reason. They wanted a broader distribution of their own stock. So they joined a larger group. Maybe also they could see down the pike when their own grandchildren might take over, and this was a cause for concern. It could be better safeguarded if the return on investment has some watchdogs in New York or Cincinnati or St. Louis.

The concept of *return on investment* as a management tool is not new. However, it is somewhat new for retailing. Most of us in distribution give Alfred P. Sloan his just due and credit. In his reorganization of the General Motors Company some fifty years ago, Mr. Sloan initiated the change in the way of evaluating the results of the company and each division by computing the relationship of profit to the real worth of invested capital. In retailing, we still have not fully appreciated the fact that net profits on sales is *not* the only gauge for success. The philosophy of Mr. Sloan was written in 1919 and can apply to the DCS of today (talking about return on investment):

"As to its bearing on organization: It increases the morale of the organization by placing each operation on its own foundation, making it feel that it is a part of the corporation assuming its own responsibility and contributing its share to the final result."

For the single-operation, owner-operated DCS, this is not so important. However, for chains it could be the start of financial success. Mr. Sloan continued:

"As to its bearing on financial control: It develops statistics correctly reflecting the relationship between the net return and the invested capital of each operating division. The true measure of efficiency—irrespective of the number of other divisions contributing thereto and the capital employed within such divisions.

As to its bearing on strategic investment: It enables the corporation to direct the placing of additional capital where it will result in the greatest benefit to the corporation as a whole."

What is the return on investment formula? There are several variations. One useful equation easily adapted is:

$$\text{ROI} = \frac{P}{S} \times \frac{S}{A} = \frac{P}{A}$$

where *ROI* is the Return on Investment; *P* is the Net Profit before taxes; *S* represents Sales; and *A* represents Assets.

Take two examples. Each yields the same ROI (a high one for retailing in general). Example 1 could be a very upgraded discount catalog showroom with a very high net profit return offering some services in elegant surroundings, fine building, and expensive location. Example 2 is a low-cost operation in a cheap building with cheap fixtures, perhaps in a low-rent district. In Example

1, the turn of merchandise is very slow. In Example 2, the merchandise is less expensive but turns rapidly. The return on investment is the same—the policy of selling and, hopefully, the original decisions were different, so that each achieved the desired results.

Example 1:

$$\frac{P}{S} = 5\%$$

$$\frac{S}{A} = 3$$

$$ROI = 15\%$$

Example 2:

$$\frac{P}{S} = 1.5\%$$

$$\frac{S}{A} = 10$$

$$ROI = 15\%$$

With calculations of this type, an established, rich company—or one requiring expensive surroundings to achieve budgeted sales—knows that markups much of the time must be extremely high and competition must not be on price when fighting low-cost stores in cheap surroundings, and vice versa.

Before progressing into further calculations and financial ratios, it is important to note that the ROI concept does not relate to dollars only, but that the figures tell the summary. Most DCS operations have—or should have—

computer assistance. Large companies have in-house computers. Small organizations must rent time and seek help from manufacturers or the coordinators.

USE OF DATA PROCESSING FOR THE DCS. This service provides:

- Sales breakdown by classification
- Analysis of merchandise received in the store by classification
- Charge and credit information with allocations properly made
- Administrative costs involved in all types of sales transactions (by analyzing and classifying transactions by merchandise)
- Investment calculation ratios regarding selling space and shelf space
- Cost sharing for space and equipment in non-selling activities (such as receiving, marking, handling)
- Sales, management, and sales-assisting employee costs including training and development.

The figures are (as always) only the beginning. After having these computer printouts or other calculations, *then* the real work begins. This is the human element. Obviously, it does no good to allocate costs to stores, departments, divisions, or even shelves unless the *people* who are in charge of these areas are involved and committed. Enter management and operatives.

In the discount catalog showroom movement, some attention has been given to training and development of

THE PEOPLE. Just as ROI relates the various financial elements of a business, the organization binds the performers. Very often, we work very hard at performing the *wrong* job. Sometimes we succeed too well in jobs we should not be doing at all. So, coordinating is the key. But for the DCS going into a larger organization, it may be too easy to go overboard. For example, the janitor should not participate in discussions regarding merchandise mix—just to use an excessive case.

However, the janitor may be included in some general meetings on merchandise plans if at all meaningful. The point to be made here is that *participative management* does not mean that everyone is involved in every decision made. Nor does it mean that decision-making conferences are just to inform the subordinates regarding the decision the top man has already made. Discount catalog showrooms, in their formative stage, already have many varying formulas, and all ideas should be considered—although not necessarily utilized. DCS is not for everyone with any system. The Dayton-Hudson and the Giant Stores experiences tell us that running a discount catalog showroom is not "a piece of cake." Today, running any retail or consumer goods business—anywhere along the channel of distribution—has enough competition to require as many scientific tools as are available.

One of these tools is ROI connected with participative management. These sophisticated tools are familiar to the larger companies in DCS. The Hudson's Bay Company of Canada, the Jewel Companies (which will have catalogs in Turn-Styles), Steinberg's (also of Canada), and certainly F. W. Woolworth (Canada Division with 10 DCS units planned) know about management tools and ROI.

There is no getting around the historical fact that early stages of a distribution formula produce returns on investment of 25 percent or higher. For one thing, the base is smaller. This is true also for earnings-to-sales ratios. Early discounters in the mid-1950s had over 20 percent ROI's and 5 percent nets. Now the figure is 12 percent for ROI and 1.5 percent or so for the net profits. But these are not problems of discounting or the discount catalog showroom alone. It could be that the DCS will survive longer in the upper brackets of both types of returns due to the lack of servicing. Wages are the real money in the inflationary spiral and also in the upgrading cycle of a formula. It may be that the DCS has become popular because there is no *bad* service to complain about and to turn customers away to other formulas. Consumer confidence in retailers—traditional retailers in general—seems to have dropped to a new low in recent years with the consumerism education. Another customer complaint that does not face the DCS to a great extent is the handling of credit and charge sales regarding returns, overdues, and so on. More than half of DCS units offer a "universal" such as Bank Americard or Master Charge.

ROI Reduced. As labor becomes more intensive, as inventories grow, and as accounts-receivable investments pile up, the return on investment is also reduced—apart from the initial start-up costs relating to the building and other things.

One temptation coming up is the problem of catalog production. *Some may be getting "too beautiful,"* which means costs go up and up. It is estimated that last year some 25 million small and large catalogs were printed (see the Appendix). This year, the figure is to be 30 percent more. Younger families as well as older ones are being introduced to the catalog through gift certificates from their companies and parents or friends. The gift certificate sales incentive is very good with salesmen. But of course the catalog must be appealing. This means cost increase— only a certain amount of which will be accepted by the customer. The rest means a lower net profit and lower ROI.

THE LITTLE GUY'S INVESTMENT. The franchise has been introduced into the formula, and the little guy who invests his savings plus his time has to get a decent salary and a higher return than in his bank account. Merchants Buying Syndicate and other big buying groups have said they feel the franchise will do well with the DCS. *Franchising as a system continues to boom* although few of us will try the Kentucky Fried Chicken or McDonald's as readily as before as the fast-food franchisee group fills in. However, the franchising movement has become more sophisticated regarding conceptual planning, adequate financial groundwork, and management training and development. ROI still remains high, too.

In 1972, franchising accounted for $141 billion in the United States and should reach $156 billion in 1973. The 1971 figure is around $128 billion. There are almost 500,000 franchised establishments in the USA. Many still have an ROI figure of over 20 percent. As far as we can gather, international franchised units reached sales of $500 million last year with the majority being in Japan, Canada, and Australia.[1] I enjoyed Kentucky Fried Chicken in New Zealand and wine at the McDonald's on the Champs Elysée in Paris just a few weeks ago.

---

[1] *National Franchise Reports* (Englewood, Colorado: Continental Reports, Inc.).

THE *POLC* FACTOR. Management is:

P   for Planning
O   for Organizing
L   for leading   (or directing if
    you prefer)
C   for controlling

In franchising, it is very easy to forget about the controlling. This is a temptation for the DCS franchise movement. It is easy to put in a mimeographed catalog and some merchandise under the name of a celebrity, and it will do well—for a few months anyway. The ROI on the first few units will be *fantastic* (know the joke, folks?), but then the fun begins when those franchisees do not get the profits projected by the franchisor.

Franchising helps the labor-intensive ROI problem. Training costs money, and the investment in people who change jobs frequently means a reduced return on investment. However, with mom and pop and granddad and grandmom on the job—to say nothing of other relatives—this cost is kept off the major problems list. There is no doubt that the DCS franchise can have all the benefits of a chain operation yet the personal warm-heart-in-the-business as well as cash benefits. Training is usually provided by the franchisor in the form of manuals, slides shows, and training films as well as live idea exchanges. Accounting and EDP services are also almost always offered by the franchisor so that ROI calculations are easily available to the small franchisee.

SOME FREE ADVICE. It has been several years since the author attended one of the first organized meetings of a franchise association. After visiting many, many, many in various countries, here is some advice. Do not take a discount catalog showroom franchise—or *any* franchise—without:

- Expecting to pay a franchise fee. People do not give away secrets in franchising.
- Thorough investigation. Pay nothing and sign nothing on the first meeting.
- For the DCS—see the catalog (is it color or black and white for instance).
- Checking all credentials and seeing at least two pilot operations.
- Planning to spend a great deal of time in the business.

The DCS Franchisor. Want to go into the discount catalog franchise business? If you have at least two operations going—why not? Your ROI from a franchisor standpoint can be 25 percent. A franchise is an agreement to exchange your know-how, name, trademarks, buying, advertising, and accounting systems as well as management development and know-how for the money and time provided by the franchisee. The contract is the thing for you. It must spell out that you will end the relationship if the franchisee violates any of the points listed. You must safeguard your name and the reputation of your trademark. You will want energetic but not necessarily experienced people:

- Who are between the ages of 25 and 70 (however, 30 to 50 is the usual).
- Who are usually married so the wife and relatives can help out.

- Who pass certain simple tests on attitudes, aptitudes, and leadership.
- Who have at least $5,000 in cash in the bank or in some cash convertible.

Some systems in the discount catalog showroom have a central distribution point so that the franchisee could have very little invested in stock (if anything except the fastest turning 100 items). Forecasting and forward planning are difficult at first, but, EDP comes in here again. Computers are available to the franchisee through the franchisor. Some more advice. The franchisor of a DCS may want to think twice before selling a franchise to an on-going company that wants to combine the DCS with an existing store or change the formula. The Giant Stores experiment (Giant Stores has the 15 or so Summit DCS units) of combinations did not work. Please remember and investigate further. On the other hand, some of the combinations are working, but it is this author's opinion that time is still needed. GEX with National Bellas Hess seems to be extremely pleased as is Giant Food in the D.C. area.

SIZE AND THE ROI FACTOR. Back to history again. The ROI was greater when the stores were smaller. It will be repeated for the DCS. But what is the solution? Competition will force the addition of more lines. Also, the Grand Distributors and others occupying large former discount stores have all the space already there anyway. Facts from the National Association of Catalog Showroom Merchandisers, Inc. (Jerome Kaufman, president), bear this out, too.

Sales up—ROI down; decide which. Very often, increased sales means reduced ROI due to duplication of services, overpurchases in fear of stockouts on a grand scale, rapid expansion in costly areas, and so on. The Carlson Company's NABS projects sales of $100 million, and this outstanding group of companies and its energetic leadership will not only achieve the sales but will probably also achieve its profits and ROI budgets. However, it could be that many companies will *sell more but enjoy it less* due to the added costs of doing business and expansion. Some optimums for good ROI's of 15 percent seem to include JEWELCOR's 25,000 square foot "ideal" with projected sales of $1.5 million the first year and $2.5 million the second year. Pilferage is to be controlled (total shrink, that is) at 1 percent. Only one of each item is on display. The desire leads the customer into the jewelry section, and the decor is built around this theme without conspicuous consumption. Low-profit merchandise is located near high-profit items. (The old island of loss surrounded by a sea of profit idea.) For a good labor "return," only 20 people, all inclusive, are utilized per shift. There is a 50-50 split (12,500 square feet in the showroom and 12,500 square feet "in the back"). Nonportable items are not carried, so there is no investment in a delivery system. The best traffic generators are located in the back, jewelry always at the entrance.

The Mini-Catalog. A good return on investment idea has been the Naum mini-catalog featuring only health and beauty aid items. The catalogs of this type are about 30 pages long. Distribution to customers is through the mail.

THE ROI TARGET. The ideal ROI varies from 10 to 15 percent. Some analysts like to have their stock-issuing companies try for 20 percent, and indeed several discount catalog showroom companies have tremendous figures reaching the 50 percent mark. Many are in the 30s and several are around 22 percent. A couple are just over 10

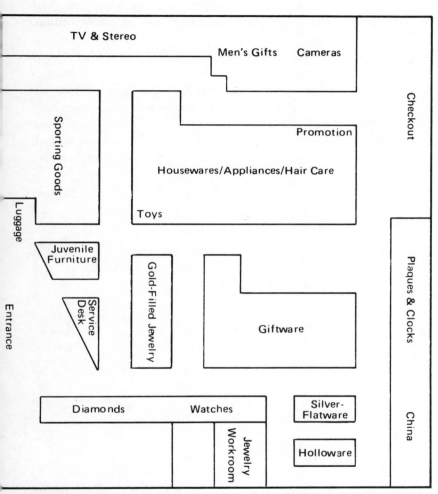

FIGURE 18 Jewelcor floor layout diagram showing location of merchandise categories. Courtesy of *Discount Store News.*

percent. Most, however, have net profits after taxes around 3.5 percent to 4 percent. Some are over 5 percent, but these are very few and as mentioned will probably remain even fewer in the future.

Another figure of importance is *revenues as a percentage of total assets*. Very often, new-formula companies have very few assets. The only thing they have are tremendous sales and net profits. However, sooner or later offices must be had, warehousing (or at least in-and-out freight transfer distribution centers), and so on are added. For many DCS companies, at present this warehouse figure is around the 2 percent to 3 percent mark.

So what is the ROI target? Just answer the questions:

- Who are my customers?
- What are my plans for expansion?
- What is the store policy regarding service and upgrading?

In other words—*need* not *greed*.

9

The Formula Spreads

The spread of discounting and of DCS's possibilities—around the world. Europeans fight back.

This page could be enlivened with a photograph of me enjoying myself at the McDonald's hamburger
fast food unit in Paris. McDonald's (with two units in and
near Paris) sells beer and wine, and the U.S. reputation
of teetotalism could be seriously endangered. However,
the important point is that even in Paris hamburgers a la
American are consumed not only by tourists but by Pari-
sians—*with a twist*. The twist (or local adaptation) is that
vin ordinaire is added to the fare. *The point is that distribution formulas spread around the world very fast.*

How Far is Too Far in Expansion? After opening those successful few discount catalog showrooms in one particular area, the successful operator has the world as his market—if not his oyster—with some careful guidelines. Some experiences and some facts could be useful to deter or encourage. In any case, the objective of this chapter is to enlighten.

Back to the hamburger—down under style. A friend from Dayton, Ohio, had sold his McDonald's franchises back to the company and headed for Australia. There, he opened some units. He has a wonderful family and a wonderful home and a wonderful yacht that he permitted me to pilot under the Sydney bridge, which entitled me to become an honorary captain in the McDonald's Australian fleet. All was well except that it seemed that business was not going to be booming as hoped. The Commodore of the fleet is no fool and had been asking his Australian friends to test the meat. In other words, the advice here is to adapt if possible and if not, get out. Sears had done as much in Australia some time earlier: it got out. However, Sears had adapted and adopted and restructured for particular localities. For example:

- Sears sells (in 1972) $10.991 billion in many areas (both geographically and line of business)
- Of this amount, $902,949,000 is done in Canada
- $206,127,000 is from Latin America
- The Spanish subsidiary rose 309.9 percent to $29.8 million in 1972 with a net profit of $1.4 million in department stores (2) and 13 sales offices.
- The Belgian subsidiary (Galleries Anspach) sold $54 million.

• Subsidiaries in Mexico and South America increased to $206.1 million, but the important point
is that net income is a high $10.2 million in 51
retail stores and 13 retail sales offices.

THE CATALOG IS THERE. So, the world is no virgin
territory as far as the catalog is concerned. It is expanding
in South Africa, too. But the opportunity of completing
the formula with the discount catalog showroom is just
beginning. On July 21, some 21 stores (or DCS's rather)
opened in the United Kingdom of Great Britain. The question is should *you* open in another country when the
United States is not yet saturated? Of course, franchising
is a possibility, and that is why the mention of McDonald's
(or for that matter KFC, which is now "everywhere," too)
and other companies. We will return to franchising, but
first let us look at the Kresge experience. It could be en-
couraging for an active, middle-size company that wants
to become a member of the billion-dollar club. A peek
also at Holiday Inns (of America, it *used* to say) will
perhaps be of some benefit.

KRESGE becomes number one after being number two
for a long, long time. Who would have guessed that earnings per share for S. S. Kresge would go from 11 cents in
1963 to more than $1.00 in 1973? Well, maybe *Chain
Store Age* did. Lebhar-Friedman Publications, Inc., copy-
righted an article in their *Variety Store/General Merchandise Executive Edition* of December 1965, entitled,
"S. S. Kresge's Restructure." At that time, the die had
been cast, and net profits had passed the $20 million mark.
But today they are over the $120 million mark. Nobody
laughs at $100 million. Certainly nobody, but nobody,
laughs at sales of $4 billion. Kresge went from $544 million in 1963 to $3.837 billion in 1972. The point of in-

terest here is the listing of two subsidiaries on the last page of the annual report:

- S. S. Kresge Company Limited, Toronto, Ontario, Canada
- K mart (Australia) Limited, Melbourne, Victoria, Australia.

Kresge-K-mart Limited, Hong Kong is so far not a retail operation. We also hear continuous rumors of K mart England, K mart Germany, and so on. A visit to the new S. S. Kresge International Headquarters, as they call it, is a delight and an artistic experience. Also visit the K marts in Australia. They are very similar to the K mart down the road from Hometown, U.S.A. Kresge executives interviewed (as early as 1961) have told me they are the world's largest discount operation with a variety store division. Their system in Australia was to join with a leading Australian operator, the G. J. Coles and Coy. variety store operation. I spoke to some 50 of their top management including their joint managing directors in Australia and again recently in the United States. K mart continues to expand using this partnership-type method. The answer here is that if a U.S.A. company does not do it, someone else will. K mart experienced this in Australia— another local company (also, like Coles, located in Melbourne) expanded very rapidly in the K mart type business. This is Target (a subsidiary of the Myer Emporium, the largest department store group in Australia with sales in the $600 million class). Lengthy interviews with the managing director of Target (who is also a Director of the Myer Group Board) revealed that Target is doing unusually well. But maybe not well enough because a third company called Venture is also doing very well in Australia. Executives of this company recently revealed tremendous expansion plans to us. By the way, Target and Venture (just like Woolworth in Australia) have no connection with their namesakes in the United States as does K mart. So, a partnership is a way for overseas expansion. Another way is the franchising method. Let us turn to the Holiday Inn story for a moment. If it works for hamburgers and chickens and discounting and motels, *why not for the discount catalog showroom,* which is as successful and as dynamic here as these formulas were when they spread across oceans.

THE WORLD'S INNKEEPERS who used to be America's innkeepers. Taken from the current annual report, we read the following, which brings joy to our heart.

"The International Peace Flag was presented by the students from four continents in the November, 1972, graduating class of Holiday Inn University (author's note: located in Olive Branch, Mississippi, 12 miles from the company headquarters in Memphis. The University is for about 5,000 persons annually to attend concentrated courses on this industry. The "University" was founded in 1959. It has 174,000 square feet with two residence halls, six lecture halls, four seminar rooms, and an amphitheater for 200, plus a 10,000-volume library.) as a tribute to Holiday Inns' aim of world understanding and friendship. It will be our goal that this flag fly at Holiday Inns throughout the world as a tangible symbol of our wish for world understanding."

The president of Holiday Inns, Inc., also wrote in this annual report that

The growth of international travel is paralleled by the expansion of the Holiday Inn System. Therefore, we of Holiday Inns commit ourselves to a policy dedicated to those acts which will enhance understanding between the peoples of the world. Our goal is expansion of the potential of goodwill among nations and encouragement of individual expressions of friendship and concord. It is our hope that through these means we may contribute to greater understanding between the peoples of the world—in the belief that through world understanding lies the way to peace for all mankind.

These people do not know when to quit. This statement was made by Jack Van Eaton, an international distribution expert regarding Holiday Inn. Indeed, we are not suggesting that the Holiday Inn companies around the world—franchising operations or company owned—will enter the discount catalog showroom industry. The point is that a little company from Memphis, Tennessee, only 20 years or so ago opened a little motel that today is located (very often via franchising) almost everywhere. This company also has expanded horizontally as well as vertically with:

- Inn Operations
- Holiday Press
- General Data
- Inn Keepers Supply Company
- Holiday Inn Food Sales
- Holiday Inn Special Products Division
- Holiday Carpet Center
- General Innkeeping Acceptance Corp.
- Holiday Manufacturing Company

- Holiday Industries
- Holiday Containers
- Artes de Mexico (furniture company)
- Holiday Inn Construction Division
- Master-Kraft Manufacturing Company
- Nat Buring Packing Company
- Johnson Furniture Company
- Marl Dinettes
- Delta Steamship Lines
- TCO Industries
- Champion Lighting Company
- Holiday Woodcraft
- Bianco Manufacturing
- International Foam

So why not add a catalog here or there???? Someone could be selling billions of dollar's, or mark's, or yen's worth of merchandise through this discount catalog show-room system.

With J. C. Penney spreading to all corners of the globe to meet Sears and other companies, it is difficult for the little guy (see chapter on return on investment), but franchising is one answer. If Holiday Inn could beat Hilton and Sheraton, why not Joe Bloke beating Sears, Penney, Kresge, or anyone from other countries—such as the Carrefours from France or the Quelles from Germany or the many, many other leading companies from all countries of the world. South Africa has been mentioned. Recently, I spoke with a very energetic lady who has started a catalog business that is growing by such leaps and bounds that she could only buy and not consider the system so much when we took her to a DCS. She said that she would have to catch up with her own mail business before expanding into a showroom, but when she does she would be back. We know she will.

I am not the only one who thinks that franchising might be the answer to foreign expansion. Below is the program from the European Franchising Symposium, which was held in October 1973.

EUROPEAN
FRANCHISING
SYMPOSIUM

organised by
BELGIAN COMMITTEE ON DISTRIBUTION
in collaboration with the
EUROPEAN FRANCHISING FEDERATION

under the patronage of
Mr. W. Claes, Minister of Economic Affairs
Mr. L. Hannotte, Minister of the Trading Classes

BRUSSELS — PALAIS DES CONGRES —
MONDAY 8 AND TUESDAY 9 OCTOBER 1973

PROGRAMME

MONDAY 8 October

Chairman: E. CATZEFLIS, president of the European Franchising Federation, Paris.

9 a.m.: *Opening of the Symposium*
Importance and development of franchising,
by the Chairman.

Franchising: a new conception of doing business,
by H. GIESEN, president, Export Marketing and Franchising A.B., general secretary of the Swedish Franchise Association (Sweden).

10.30: Coffee break

11: *The basis of franchising: the contract. Practical legal aspects,*
by G. G. ABELN, barrister, secretary of the Dutch Franchising Federation, Rotterdam (Netherlands).

Franchising and pyramid selling,
by J. O. GOUGH, director, Kleeneze Holdings Ltd, Bristol (Great Britain).

Discussion

1 p.m.: Luncheon

2.30: *The practical development of a franchise. Part I. Three case studies.*

Frantel (hotel chain),
by M. LABILLE, general manager, Frantel, Paris (France).

Ascot (dry cleaning),
by F. W. J. SCHALEN, director, European franchising consultants, Soesterberg (Netherlands).

Moderne Bauelemente (complete solution for construction problems),
by H. BOEHM, franchising expert, Munich (Germany).

4: Coffee break

4.30: *Franchising and European law. Articles 85 and 86 of the Treaty of Rome: no incompatibility,*
by M. BROSSOLET, barrister, Paris (France).

The financing of a franchise,
by A. F. KELLER, management consultant, franchising expert, president of the Swiss franchising Federation, Berne (Switzerland).

Discussion

TUESDAY 9 October

Chairman: J. BAPTIST, member of the board and general secretary, Comité Belge de la Distribution, Brussels.

9 a.m.: *Brand, sign, name, image: valuable capital. How can they be protected?*
by W. SKAUPY, franchising expert, Munich (Germany).

Franchising: new possibilities for the small and medium-sized firms and a new orientation for the voluntary chains,
by J. KNIGGE, consultant, Service & Franchise project partner, Munich (Germany).

Franchising also possible for large-surface enterprises,
by M. WEILL, research director, Centre universitaire de Toulon (France).

11: Coffee break

11.30: *How to recruit a franchisee?*
by M. LUCAS, general manager, Lévitan, Paris (France).

Franchising trade fairs. Excellent recruiting medium,
by R. JANSSENS, consultant, Comité Belge de la Distribution, Brussels (Belgium).

Discussion

1 p.m.: Luncheon

2.30: *The practical development of a franchise. Part II.*
Three case studies.

Christiaensen (toys' shops)
by G. CHRISTIAENSEN, manager, N. V. Christiaensen, Aartselaar (Belgique).

Crysalid (ladies' boutiques)
by C. G. SEROUDE, president of the Group Epac International, Franchise development consultants, Paris (France).

Wimpy (fast food),
by P. R. ENSDORFF, managing director, Wimpy service Benelux B.V., Amsterdam (Netherlands).

4.15: Coffee break

4.45: *The franchisee's bible. Things to think of before signing a contract,*
by E. CATZEFLIS

Discussion

Conclusions of the Symposium.

PRACTICAL INFORMATION

Dates: Monday 8 and Tuesday 9 October 1973.

Place: Palais des Congrès, Benelux Hall, rue Ravenstein, Brussels.

Languages: Simultaneous interpretation in English, French, Dutch and German.

Parking facilities:
Parking Albertine, entrance: rue des Sols, and place de la Justice.

Registration for Symposium:
By means of the enclosed form, accompanied by a transfer order or cheque made out to the Société Générale de Banque (Postal cheque account No. 2.61), Brussels, for account No. 210.0964970-66 of the Comité Belge de la Distribution, Brussels.
Participation fee: 4.000 BF + 720 BF (VAT) + 700 BF (luncheons, VAT included) = 5.420 BF.
The fee covers: participation in the sessions
provision of documentation
luncheons
coffee.

Accommodation:
Please apply to the Agence Lissone-Lindeman, rue des Colonies 58, 1000 Brussels (Tel. 02/13 06 58 and 13 09 83, Telex 22604) which has reserved rooms for the benefit of participants.

Further information from:
Comité Belge de la Distribution, rue Saint-Bernard 60, 1060 Brussels—Tel. 02/38 41 14.

A TWO-WAY AIRWAY. For many years, Americans have been exporting ideas as well as merchandise. Now, however, we are importing all items. Takashimaya has long operated on New York's Fifth Avenue. Other overseas companies continue to make inroads. Sears will not go out of business due to Quelle's U.S. catalog promotions. But Sears sells less (as a percentage, that is) via catalog than in the past. So, in addition to looking across the ocean for greener pastures, keep an eye out for some foreign invasions, too.

INVASION OF U.S. BY FOREIGN FIRMS SPEEDS UP

Never in history have foreign business enterprises engaged in such a headlong rush to *buy out or into American* business as today. This also includes production and distribution facilities.

Close to 600 foreign firms already have direct investments in the United States, holdings which add up to more than *15 billion dollars.* This is a relatively small figure when compared with the *$90* billion of American holdings abroad—but the *gap is closing.*

Spurring the trend is the capability of businessmen all over the world to *equal if not surpass* American products in design and quality at comparable and often lower prices.

Add to this the view people everywhere have of America as a huge market with *unlimited potential,* and it's not difficult to see why foreign firms are eager to get a *bigger piece* of this huge rich pie than would be attainable through exports alone.

Furthermore, the continuing weakness of the dollar —on top of two devaluations in 14 months—tempts foreign firms to *take advantage* of what they see as bargain basement prices for acquisitions.

BENEFIT TO U.S.

Keen observers of the multinational invasion, now underway, predict that one benefit, at least short term, will be an *improvement* of the U.S. balance of trade. As an opener, they point out the deficit in our trade balance has shrunk from $6 billion in 1972 to a current slight surplus.

As Fortune magazine says: "The flow of European and Japanese capital to the U.S. should be increasing. Foreign companies are quickly learning to unravel the hitherto baffling mysteries of the inviting U.S. market."

To the American marketer, this overseas desire to *get into the action* here through direct involvement presents many marketing problems which will demand new solutions and innovative counteracting strategy.

A brief glance at what's happening.

JAPAN FIRST AND FOREMOST

First and foremost in this quest for direct action by acquiring a piece of America's business world is Japan. U.S. News and World Report states: "The Japanese are not coming, they're here—buying into companies and purchasing plants, leasing timber, looking over mining properties, accumulating hotels and snapping up real estate."

A few specifics.

- Most recent is the purchase by Japanese Mitsui & Co., Ltd., of a major interest in American Metal Climax Inc.

- Toyota Motor Sales U.S.A. Inc. and Chinook Motor Lodge signed an agreement to produce and market a *compact motor home* here.

- An *industrial park* financed by Japanese interests will be built in Charlotte, North Carolina.

- The Meiwa Gravure Chemical Company will build a factory to produce *printed vinyl chloride tablecloths* in Charlotte and phase out exporting this item to the U.S. from Japan.

- YKK Zipper Co. will build a zipper plant in Georgia.

- Japan International Technology Corporation will seek to acquire American companies marketing electronics and precision metal products.

- Palace Hotel in San Francisco, formerly a Sheraton property, has been *acquired by* the Kokusai Kogyo Company.

- A new industrial development in Irvine, California, will house the national headquarters of Mazda Motors of America as well as *manufacturing* complexes and *distribution* facilities of *other* Nipponese companies.

- In addition, Japanese firms are *already* turning out television sets, chemicals, electronics and are preparing to produce *steel* in an Auburn, N.Y. mill.

ACTIONS FROM OTHER LANDS

Following on the heels of the busy Japanese are actions by companies from *other lands* like these:

- A Norwegian *ship owner* is trying to acquire the Zapata Corporation.

- Plans for a huge complex in South Carolina are in progress by Michelin, the French *tire manufacturer*.

- Volvo is reported to be contemplating the construction of a multimillion dollar *assembly plant* in Virginia.

- Siemens Corporation of Germany has acquired Computest Corporation in New Jersey as part of a *long-range plan* to buy other companies.

- England is also *on the move*. The influential British magazine, The Economist, advises: "Now is the time to invade the United States."

- The invasion is already *underway*. Typical recent happenings: Lloyds of London Bank seeks the First Western Bank and Trust Co. of California.

- British Land Company made a bid for the Uris Building Corporation.

In addition to invading the American business world by acquiring or building production and distribution facilities, foreign companies are *pouring money* into investments in American business.

There is a tremendous *surplus of dollars* floating around Europe, and overseas banks are eager to lend them for investment in America.

Ronson Corporation, maker of cigarette lighters, electric shavers and other electricals, has been fighting a *take-over* by Liquifin Aktiengesellschaft.

Stauffer's food processing and restaurant chain subsidiary of Litton Industries, *is being acquired* by Nestle, the Swiss-owned food firm.

SURPRISE IN RETAILING

But the most surprising aspect of the marketing invasion of America is what's going on in the *retail field.*

The acquisition of *Gimbels department store* chain by Brown & Williamson, a United States subsidiary of British-American Tobacco, is well known. The business world regards this move as an effort to widen B.A.T.'s profit base by becoming a potent force in world retailing.

America's *Franklin Stores Corporation* is now owned by *Hill Samuel, the British banking organization,* through the purchase of a stock majority. This also puts the ownership of *Barker's discount chain in British hands.* It is reported that this is but the *first step* of a plan to expand the operations of this British company by the acquisition of other American firms, not necessarily retail.

Perhaps the most ambitious program to invade American retailing is the announced entrance into the

United States of Carrefour, French version of an American *discount chain.*

Carrefour has been making *great strides* throughout Europe with its "hypermarché" super stores, which combine general merchandise and foods. An idea of the magnitude of these stores can be gleaned from the new 250,000 square foot store in Toulouse, France, expected to do $50 million a year: 60 percent in food and 40 percent in all other categories.

Carrefour is planning a "hypermarché" in Canada, Canadian competitors have already *anticipated this move.* Toronto-based *Oshawa*, operator of discount department stores, is set to open a 250,000 square foot "hypermarché" *in Laval.* Steinberg's, operating *34 full-line discount stores in Quebec and Ottawa,* is readying three "hypermarché" type units.

Even though Carrefour's key executives say that everything their company has learned is from American chains, the French firm has *added many innovations* in areas ranging from display to merchandising.

U.S. MARKETERS MUST PREPARE TO COPE

As the invasion of the United States by European and Asian marketers speeds up, it becomes urgent for American business to examine marketing and advertising policies to cope with it.

Awareness is the first step. Each company will want to be fully informed as to what's going on and to evaluate the probable effects of the flood tide of competition from abroad.

Not only on our national economy, but on its specific industry and/or on the company's own business.

Some questions:

Do the invasive actions by the foreign marketers forecast a long-term flow of capital, as Forbes magazine puts it, that will in part offset the strength of the U.S. multinational corporations abroad? Forbes says: *"The answers aren't in yet."*

How will the increased number of overseas competitors in the U.S. market affect *new product developments?* It has already influenced the automobile industry.

In many cases, United States companies also bring home technology developed by their *subsidiaries abroad.* Examples: Gillette's Trac II razor and National Cash Register's electronic register 230.

Will protectionist government policies—once powerful, always latent—be rekindled, and block invading capital or the expatriation of profits?

Will we make it easy or difficult for foreign labor to work in foreign-controlled businesses here? To what extent will the "invading capital" help in easing our own unemployment problem?

Will the rotation of added thousands of executives from the mother countries to the U.S. and back create a greater fondness for American products and thus have a *positive effect* on our exports . . . and balance of payments?

How will the invasion affect the *advertising* business? Will it intensify client conflict situations? Will overseas agencies come here in greater numbers?

Some advertising practitioners say that their foreign counterparts have caught up with creativity in advertising which was once considered "almost an American monopoly." Will *advertising creativity* in the U.S. be affected?

Will foreign media publish American editions in English of prestigious foreign publications such as The London Times, German Der Spiegel, French Le Monde, Japanese Asahi Shimbun?

Will the invading companies bring new techniques of sales promotion? There is already considerable evidence that the "hypermarchés" have developed some *highly effective retail promotion ideas.*

What action is likely from the U.S. *government* which will seriously affect marketing and advertising?

These are but a few of the questions which will arise as the invasion gathers speed.

Alert businessmen are already pondering these *imponderables and others.*[1]

[1] Pages 131–137 reprinted by permission from "Grey Matter —Thoughts and Ideas on Advertising and Marketing," Vol. 44, No. 9, September 1973, published by Grey Advertising Inc., 777 Third Avenue, New York, New York 10017.

10

The Fast
and Furious Future of DCS

FIFO. Fast in, fast out could be the plan for some discount catalog showroom operators. At recent meetings and conventions where the discount catalog showroom has been a very hot topic, some experts have reported a very short life cycle for the DCS formula. This could be the case as the formula now stands. However, like all formulas (the department store started in 1852 by Aristede Boucicaut with his Bon Marché in Paris has changed; the supermarket started by perhaps Michael Cullen in his King Kullen stores in New York; the self-service, checkout discount department store formula perhaps organized by Marty Chase in his ANN & HOPE, and so on), the discount catalog showroom will change. Early tests have already changed (or some have closed).

The reason for the closings are as varied as the reasons for success. See the Appendix for the pitfalls. Combinations and recombinations are already appearing.

Miracle Mart. This company feels that adjacent showrooms to their self-service discount department stores is the answer.

GEX. This company already has tried incorporating a showroom store in the conventional GEX membership discount department store.

Fred. The Fred Meyer group in Portland, Oregon, has announced catalog showrooms and home improvement centers and the possibility of future combinations with supermarkets, drug stores, and discount department stores. They have been encouraged by the success of their home center experiment of a few years.

THE CATALOG. Anyone can put a catalog in his shop. Indeed, many do and will increase assortment by doing just this. It is now almost possible to get anything at any place. The decision is depth, price, delivery desired, and convenience—mainly the time factor. Do you want it now, in a little while, tomorrow, or when?

The Giants. Giant and Giant Food have already been mentioned. The president of Giant Food has said that all Giant units will have at least a catalog book and order desk. The complete DCS we visited in Virginia was very well done. For the supermarket operator (A&P, Kroger, *et al.*, take note), this could be IT.

Super Valu. Green Bay and Marshfield are having 30,000 square feet discount catalog showrooms next to existing ShopKo units. Can you see a real warehouse DCS in a Super Valu distribution center??? This could really have *everything for everybody under one roof.*

Wickes. This conglomerchant had barely settled down in the booming home center or DIY (Do It Yourself) formula when furniture warehouse showrooms developed. The catalog showroom is easily attached.

The Hi-Lo Theory. Pile it high and sell it low (cheap) has been a pillar of the supermarket, SSDDS, and discount formula. Max Zimmerman, the late founder of the Super Market Institute and author on this topic, has sat in my office for hours expounding this and saying that the surroundings must be pleasant and not "slaughter houses," as he put it. The DCS does not pile it at all—the store is indeed a very pleasing place.

THE PRESENT IS NO GUIDE FOR THE FUTURE. After studying discount catalog showroom combinations in various areas of the country and discussing the formula with distribution leaders, the conclusion is to try it with any combination that makes sense for you. This could be the corner grocery, gas station, discount store or specialist in any line of business. One-stop shopping has been a trend that may now be on the wane so that the formula for the DCS of 1975 may be completely different from that of the present discount catalog showrooms. The hypermarket development, a recession, inflation in food prices, and many other socioeconomic trends will make an impact on the final form the DCS will take. But this has been the case with the supermarket, the shopping center, and the discount house.

EMAC. The enclosed mall air-conditioned center we now love so much on those snowy, rainy, or hot days when the temperature is 72 degrees inside the place seems to indicate that the housewife makes two shopping trips that are distinctly different. On one, she is shopping for fashion and specialty items. During the other, she is shopping for staples and basic needs. Consequently, the EMAC we see going up today has no supermarket although regional malls of recent vintage had three supermarkets. Now the EMAC has five department stores and the supermarket is not even in the enclosed part of the center but off the parking lot to one side. In theory, the housewife or the consumer in general (the housewife still spends over 80 percent of our retail dollar) wants to have and to hold the desired and desirable merchandise as quickly as possible. Hence, *one-stop shopping makes real sense.* But we are not logical people. Don't we always try to get something for nothing and many times end up paying a great deal more than we should? And also don't we go to shops to just do exactly that—shop? Think again of "If they can't steal it . . . they can't buy it either."

Sorry folks—no guide yet. To sum up this brief line of thought, it seems that the future of the DCS will be a long one. There is always a market even for buggy whips. It is limited, but I am told (not by Secretariat) that today there are more horses in the United States than in the "horse and buggy" days. However, that exact formula of mix, size, location is not yet established.

11

The Post Postface

THE FUTURE IS ALWAYS THE QUESTION. What is the future of retailing and what is the discount catalog's place in this future? Many people think that retailing will be over the $500 billion mark very soon and that just over $110 billion will be for food and drink. The remaining merchandise can easily be sold via some part of the discount catalog showroom formula. The National Association of Catalog Showroom Merchandisers (NACSM) is listing some 1,200 companies with almost 2,000 showrooms. Most companies have just a few branches at the moment. Discount houses or SSDDS rose from 1,000 to more than 6,000 and some $27 billion (or more than department stores) in just a few years.[1]

[1] *Statistical Abstract of the United States, 1973* (Washington, DC.: Department of Commerce, Government Printing Office, 1973), pp. 476, 738, 741.

SAVINGS. It is the savings that the customer is after. The most efficient type of distribution can give the lowest prices. In addition, the DCS has the expertise of the co-ordinator company, such as Creative Merchandising, Srago, Mutual, Progressive, American Merchandisers, Dahnken (of Salt Lake City), Arm (New York), Warren Abbey of Cleveland, Basic, Tempco, Ken Klassics, Paul Schultz, Federated, Comprehensive, Gordon of Houston, Wilson from the Zale Corp., Douglas Lehrman, etc., etc. Also, "old timers," such as Medco, Zale, Gold Bond Stamp Co., Malone & Hyde, Volume Merchandise, and Vornado, are going in or have gone in with all information and imagination required to keep this infant industry alive and offering the lowest prices in town on the best value merchandise. The U.S. Department of Commerce says that by 1980 the total of retail sales will be more than $725 billion. The DCS expansion will be eyeing this increase with no traditions telling the DCS operator that he cannot get these extra billions of dollars.

INFLATION AND CATALOGS. Income levels are rising and the projected average family income of $15,000 of 1980 or 1990 [2] will also mean that now there are substantial dollars to work with. The family will be better educated to saving as much as possible so that leisure activities and additional goods can be purchased. Mechanization/automation is already being studied for the DCS. The first mention of the March 1973 *Catalog and Showroom Merchandiser*, Volume 1, Number 7, is concerned with warehousing, financing, shrinkage (shortages), and education.

The Specialist and the Mass Merchandiser. Some specialization is already appearing. However, a catalog only

[2] U.S. Bureau of the Census, *Current Population Reports,* Series P. 23.

for cookware, only for jewelry, or a DCS with only one line is certainly a possibility that could grow into national proportions so that style as well as savings could be offered the very discriminating customer. Some specialists say they could join the move but want to see the outcome of the dispute over catalog price coding. *The Discount Merchandiser* survey indicates that most operators and soon-to-be operators are not worried. Most answered that they will continue to use coding until it is "outlawed."

THE SHAKEOUT has been much discussed by the people watching the development of the DCS. The report in the January issue of *Women's Wear Daily* on the presentation of Jack H. Shapiro of Giant Stores Corp. (Chelmsford, Massachusetts) at the National Retail Dry Goods Association session in New York shows that a maturity of the DCS is a long way off. In the meantime, Giant's earlier announcement of its opening of 20 Summit DCS units is being appraised. Other experts, such as Top Value Enterprises, Inc., operator of some 500 trading stamp outlets in the United States, seem ready to expand rapidly into the DCS line.

SOME LIKE IT COOL. After the initial thrust, there is also the "conversion" technique in the DCS future. When any softgoods or general merchandise (SSDDS for example) store is not too satisfied with its sales and profit performance, there is always the conversion into a DCS such as Service Merchandise (Zayre and J. B. Hunter–Almart of Louisville, and so on) and Zayre are doing. Zayre has its Volume Impact Products program. VIP can go many ways for Zayre, and certainly the conversion is open to Grant, Woolco and how about K mart. Sooner or later, some of the 500 might be slowing down and changing from K marts to a "K DCS."

Shades of William H. Albers. If I remember Max Zimmerman correctly, Mr. Albers left the presidency of Kroger because he wanted to open his own chain of supermarkets. Mr. Bullock (Burley Bullock) is the former head of Zale's leased department division but is now the new president of Bullock's Catalog Showcase. Other leaders take note—and start your own company. Why not?

The Bullock DCS group is to be in the south Texas area (the first is in Corpus Christi's Ayres shopping center). The company will use the Giant Food catalog, which is said to be the catalog for Jewel's TurnStyle DCS and Howard Brothers and some food chains that plan DCS operations.

Unending Combinations may also be in the future of the DCS. There is a very hot expansion program in the furniture warehouse showroom and the Home Center Showroom. Will Levitz, Wickes, Lowe's, Evans Products, Builders Emporium open with a separate DCS unit? There are SSDDS's with furniture warehouses that have catalogs already. And then there is the shopping center question. Will new (regional EMACs, community, or neighborhood) shopping centers open with a DCS unit? There are some 15,000 shopping centers in the United States with only a few now offering the DCS, and most of these are the smallest type.

The National Observer of May 12, 1973 (page 9), brings up the question of service. For example: is a jeweler on hand and does the DCS do its clock repair, TV repair, and so on. This question need not color the future of the DCS because the SSDDS answered it some time ago— and the manufacturer wants to stay in business, too. The DCS business is a name brand business at the moment. Wholesalers come into the picture as well as manufacturers, and both may open DCS outlets. In Miami, for example, Luria and Sons—former wholesalers—have done just that.

WORK AND ADVERTISE. Value House of Lewiston, Maine has television spots 52 weeks of the year, and certainly advertising will play a part of the future of the success of the DCS. However, as the *National Observer* observed, "You've got to know your territory." Anyone who does not know and love retailing will have a hard time succeeding with the DCS just as he did with the SSDDS, department store, and supermarket. But there is a great future here, and all of us will be watching, waiting, and rooting.

Appendix

DCS Guide and Reference

Mail Order Business Directory. Although the discount catalog showroom is a long way from the mail order house, the number of both seem to be increasing daily. The last *Complete Guide to the Mail Order Market* (you can get this from B. Klein Publications, Inc., 11 3rd Street, Rye, N.Y. 10580), that I could put my hands on lists some 5,000 mail order firms.

This chapter will by no means be complete but will list by company the important decisions regarding "how it is done" by DCS firms. Some of these how-to decisions vary greatly. For example, one firm—MacDonald—uses newspaper ads to publicize specials. Others feel that "special value" catalog supplements, sent directly to their

mailing list customers, have more impact. At this stage
of the DCS developmental cycle, I feel it is useless as
well as misguiding for anyone to say that one way is
better than another. Customer segmentation, management abilities, financial structuring, local competitive con-
ditions, pricing policies, and other factors determine these
variances. Trial and error is not the least important among
these "other factors," either, which is why no one can yet
say, "this is the way to do it." Every firm is still trying new
variations. In addition, a listing of stores and locations
in a new and developing line of business can never be
complete. This is the excitement of a new business. However, it is useful to know locations and other information
about DCS units so that you can visit or inquire. In any
case, you will want to know how leading DCS companies
handle certain problems and activities. This is the objective of this appendix.

Consequently, the information about the companies'

- History
- Headquarters
- Procedures
- Store locations
- Policy decisions

is to serve as a guide to companies of varying sizes and
location. It is to be a guide and reference—nothing more.

Company, Headquarters, Other Locations	Size of Units	Catalog and Inventory	Sales and Profits	Other Information

BASCO (10)
Chestnut Street,
Philadelphia, Pa.
California:
  Santa Anna
Pennsylvania:
  Montgomeryville *
  Philadelphia
  Pittsburgh
	25,000 sq. ft.-
	32,000 sq. ft.
		Uses Creative Merchandising catalog	1972
			  $13,400,000
			1973
			  $21,000,000	

W. BELL & COMPANY (9)
12401 Twinbrook
  Parkway
Rockville, Md. 20852
Georgia:
  Atlanta (1)
Maryland:
  Baltimore-Washington,
  D.C. area (6)
Texas:
  Houston (2)
	30,000 sq. ft., total;
	10,000 sq. ft., showroom
		Uses its own 304-page
		  catalog.
			1972
			  $15,800,000
			1973
			  $20,000,000	

Numbers in parentheses following company names are total number of units. Others are number of units in specified locations.
* Future location now being developed.

Company, Headquarters, Other Locations	Size of Units	Catalog and Inventory	Sales and Profits	Other Information
BEST PRODUCTS COMPANY, Inc. (29)	50,000 sq. ft. is average; 60,000 sq. ft. is prototype for new suburban solo location. This type is usually 2-floors, with 20,000 sq. ft. showroom. 40% is showroom space; 60% warehouse.	Creative Merchandising catalog: 450 pages; more than 350,000 of these are mailed once a year with seasonal and sale supplements sent during the year. Vendors assist with printing and mailing costs.	1972 $51,800,000	Average showroom has 10 full-time and 60 part-time employees who work 10-30 hours per week.
U.S. Highway No. 1			1973 $103,000,000	
Ashland, Va. 23005				Advertising cost per showroom is 2% of sales.
California:			Net Profits	
Campbell-Cupertino			1972	
Sacramento (2)			$1,700,000	
San Jose *				
Ohio:			Average annual sales per unit—	
Akron			$7,000,000	
Cleveland				
Dayton		Sells 10,000 nationally advertised products; 75% of merchandise is under complete EDP control. Items ordered by mail, phone or in showroom. Has 2 Distribution centers (Richmond, Va. and Dallas, Tex.)		
Toledo				
Maryland:				
Baltimore				
Carrollton				
Rockville				
Michigan:				
Flint				
North Carolina:				
Durham				
Fayetteville				
Raleigh				

Pennsylvania:
Allentown *
Harrisburg *
Texas:
Amarillo
Austin
Corpus Christi
Dallas
Houston
Lubbocks
San Antonio
Witchita Falls
Virginia:
Arlington
Falls Church
Hampton
Lynchburg
Richmond
Roanoke
Virginia Beach

| CENTURY HOUSEWARES (35) P.O. Box 35 Buffalo, N.Y. 14240 Indiana (cont'd.) | 51,000 sq. ft., prototype opened in Springfield, Ohio; 14,000 sq. ft.- 28,000 sq. ft., average | Has its own 260-page catalog | 1972 | $39,500,000 | During 1973, a unit in Dayton, Ohio closed. It was in a community shopping center, in a former clothing store of 30,000 sq. ft. |

* Future locations now being developed.

153

Company, Headquarters, Other Locations	Size of Units	Catalog and Inventory	Sales and Profits	Other Information
CENTURY HOUSEWARES (cont.) Michigan New York Ohio Pennsylvania				
CONSUMERS DISTRIBUT- ING (82) Toronto, Canada Connecticut (1) Long Island, N.Y. (5) Queens, N.Y. (1) New Jersey (1) San Francisco Bay area (10) Ontario, Canada	11,00 sq. ft., total; 4,000 sq. ft. showroom space. Some are smaller; most located in shopping centers.	Central distribution center and owns fleet of trailers to distribute to branches; system is computerized.	1972 $50,000,000 5% net profits	Owned by May Department Stores of St. Louis, Mo., and Consumers Distributing, Ltd., Canada
DAHNKEN (48) Salt Lake City, Utah Arizona California Colorado Nevada New York City Oregon	6,000 sq. ft.- 12,000 sq. ft.	Has its own 335-page catalog, which is is- sued every September.	1973 $35,000,000	Forty-five of the Dahnken units are franchises. Franchisees pay an initial fee and a per- centage of the gross of each unit. For this, Dahnken pro- vides the use of its name, catalog, and coordinator ser- vices. Investment capital is

Texas Utah Washington			$75,000 to $100,000. New units usually open in September to coincide with issuing of new catalog.

ELLMAN'S (3)
Atlanta, Georgia
All units in Atlanta
	67,800 sq. ft., total;
	50,000 sq. ft. for ware-
	  housing
		Has its own 400-page
		  catalog.
			1972
			$11,000,000
			1973
			$17,000,000
			Net Profits
			1972
			$762,000

ESCO (9)
6545 Carnegie Avenue
Cleveland, Ohio 44103
Ohio:
  Akron
  Cleveland
  Middletown
	17,000 sq. ft., total;
	7,000 sq. ft, for show-
	  room; 10,000 sq. ft.
	  for warehouse
		Uses Comprehensive
		  Catalog.
			Formerly the Economy Sales Co.;
			is now part of Louis Schaffer
			Diversified.

GIANT FOODS (4)
Landover, Md.
Washington, D.C. area
		Prepares its own 384-
		  page catalog.
		
		Inventory is computer
		  controlled.
			Now also operating as catalog coordinator; but no merchandise advising. Three other chains with 11 units use this catalog—Turn-Style (part of Jewel), Bullocks, and S.M.R.

Company, Headquarters, Other Locations	Size of Units	Catalog and Inventory	Sales and Profits		Other Information
GRAND DISTRIBUTORS (9) Elmwood Park, N.J.	30,000 sq. ft., total for prototype; 15,000 sq. ft. each, showroom and warehouse	Uses Jewelcor catalog			Division of Grand Union's Stop & Save Trading Stamp Company

JEWELCOR (14)
New York
Florida:
  Jacksonville *
Indiana:
  Indianapolis *
New Jersey:
  Pleasentville *
Pennsylvania:
  Harrisburg *
  Scranton *
  York *
	25,000 sq. ft.-
	30,000 sq. ft.
		Has its own 392-page catalog (also one with shortened toy section of 360 pages). Put out 2 supplements in 1973; 5 supplements to go out in 1974.	1972
			1973
				$54,800,000
				$80,000,000
					Jewelcor also has joint venture with W. T. Grant called Granjewel.
					
					A number of showrooms use Jewelcor's catalog; it will send out 5,000,000 books in 1974. It charges its own showrooms 80 cents a book and other showrooms $1.00 to $1.20 a book (depending on how many books are ordered).

E. F. MacDONALD (2) 129 S. Ludlow Street Dayton, Ohio	22,400 sq. ft.	Puts out a 350-page catalog once a year. Member of Jewelcor and Srago of Miami buying group.	1971	$244,900,000	Mainly engaged in creation and administration of incentive programs and the licensing and administration of trading stamp plan (Plaid Stamps). Thirty employees—up to 60 employees at peak periods.

MAMMOTH MART, INC.
321 Manley Street
West Bridgewater, Mass.
02379

This company is a leader in the self-service discount department store field. Total company sales for year ending Feb. 3, 1973 were more than $158,000,000. In 1972, Mammoth Mart opened a KEY DCS outside of Boston, but due to a loss in this new venture it closed in September, 1973. It is not planning to reopen in this field—it rented the space to an apparel store.

MODERN MERCHAN-	50,000 sq. ft., average	Uses and publishes Creative Merchandising catalog.
DISE (22)		
Meadowbrook Office		1972 $42,000,000
Plaza		1973 $90,000,000
6490 Excelsior Boulevard		
St. Louis Park, Minn.		

FRED MEYER, INC. (4)
Washington:
Portland
Seattle

17,000-20,000 sq. ft.

Uses catalog of Mutual Merchandising Cooperative

This is a new venture for one of the biggest food and general merchandising chains in the northwest.

NAUM BROS., INC. (7)
2373 Ridge Road West
Rochester, N.Y. 14626
New York:
Chili
Greece Towne Mall
Lackawanna
Southfield
Syracuse
Webster

42,000 sq. ft., average total;
20,000 sq. ft. for show-room

Uses Creative Merchandising catalog.

1972 $14,100,000
1973 $24,000,000

Self-service is used in games, sporting goods, hardware, and health and beauty aids departments.

* Future locations now being developed.

Company, Headquarters, Other Locations	Size of Units	Catalog and Inventory	Sales and Profits	Other Information
SAM SOLOMON COM-PANY (5) Charleston, S.C.	80,000 sq. ft., average total	Uses MAI (Merchandisers Association Inc.) cata-log, which has 500 pages.	1972 $10,000,000 1973 $18,000,000 1974 (projected) $30,000,000	

SERVICE MERCHAN-DISING (18)
481 McNally Drive
Nashville, Tenn. 37211
Alabama:
  Huntsville *
  Montgomery *
Georgia:
  Atlanta
Indiana:
  Indianapolis *
Ohio:
  Cincinnati
  Columbus
	60,000 sq. ft.-80,000 sq. ft.;60,000 sq. ft. is total for prototype; of this, 27,000 sq. ft. is show-room and 33,000 sq. ft. is warehouse	Uses Creative Merchan-dising catalog; also uses TRU specials cata-log and has a spring and summer supple-ment.
		
		Showrooms display 120,000 items.
			1973
			$40,000,000
			Net Profit
			$1,200,000
				Twelve units are in former dis-count department stores; most new units are near interstate highways or belt systems.
				
				Credit sales amounted to 20% in 1973.
				
				Advertising is 2% of sales.
				
				Has 10 full-time and 60 part-time employees in each unit; they work from 10 to 40 hours per week. Each store has manager and co-manager.

Oklahoma:
Tulsa
Tennessee:
Carlotte
Chatanooga
Memphis
Nashville
Whitehaven *

VALUE HOUSE (13)	35,000 sq. ft., average total	Uses 300-page Creative Merchandising catalog.	1973 $35,000,000 1974 (projected) $65,000,000	Owned by Supermarkets General Corp., which also owns Rickel Home Center and Pathmark
Lewiston, Maine				
Connecticut (2)				
Long Island, N.Y. (1)				
Maine (6)				
New Hampshire (4)				

*Future locations now being developed.

More on Present and Future Units

Best is the largest DCS, according to a report by Smith, Barney and Company (1345 Avenue of the Americas, New York, N.Y. 10019). Store organization gives the manager overall responsibility for operations, cost control, customer relations, merchandising displays as well as training. Managers have two or three years experience with Best. They are paid salary and bonus. The bonus is tied to profitability, and the average manager makes between $20,000 and $30,000. Under him are the assistant manager, four department heads, and a warehouse manager. During peak periods, some 150 people work at a typical Best unit. At slow times, 50 people work—25 are full time.

The Best Building. The company usually leases the land, the buildings, and the fixtures. Capital requirements are:

- Land—over $200,000
- Building—around $1,000,000
- Fixtures—about $250,000
- Inventory—approximately $1,000,000

In June 1973, total Best showroom space was over 1 million square feet. By the end of June 1974, the total showroom space will be 1.5 million square feet. And, the average sales per square foot is around $110.00 (see the profit figures on the chart and below).

Few companies ever state to themselves (or to their suppliers, employees, or customers) exactly what the goals and policies and procedures are, at least not out loud. Of course, change and rapid change could make a policy statement meaningless. For example, many stores have opened in barns and shifted to palaces. Others have started with 100 percent self-service, checkout systems and have moved to a service environment. Others have gone from cash and carry to credit and delivery: It is interesting to recall that the now $5 billion J. C. Penney company has offered credit for only some 15 years.

The DCS policy is usually set in general terms along broad lines. Strengths and weaknesses of buildings and procedures—as well as management and employee talent —are usually also known even if not stated. This is also true of booklets and outlines covering procedures and policies. Few are in manual form, but the guidelines are accepted and understood verbally. Training, communications, motivational thrusts, measurements, and standards are also not yet so established. On the other hand, management and employees are encouraged to take risks, expand creatively, and set their own goals.

Best and the Attitude Survey. The Best emphasis is on change for the better. A form at the catalog desk says, "Our President would like your comments," and a no-postage, moisten-at-the-top-seal form lists five questions, which ask for a yes or no answer, plus allowing space for additional comments and suggestions. The questions are:

- Did you find what you were looking for?
- Had you selected an item from our catalog before you came into our showroom?
- Did you look at non-catalog items after you came in?
- Did you notice our "tru-specials"? (In some

stores, some space is also given to "Red Arrow reduced specials.")

- What other types of merchandise would you like Best Products to handle?

There is also space to list name and address "if you wish." The form also asks the customer if she has a catalog, and if not, says that for $1.00, she will be put on the mailing list.

The Best Card. At the time of purchase, the customer must present a card issued by Best. The card mentions that it remains "the property of Best Products Co., Inc., Richmond, Va., and it may be cancelled at any time." The card lists Best Products as Catalog Distributors and Manufacturers Agents. The reverse side has a statement of Best Product Company's policies:

1. To sell goods to merchants who purchase for resale, also to business firms, organizations, and institutions who purchase for gifts, prizes, premiums, incentive awards, etc. To build employee morale, our customers may also authorize their employees to purchase from our catalog and to visit our Showrooms.

2. Any individual who obtains a Showroom Admission Card by means of giving false or misleading information will cause admission privileges to be revoked. Only a holder of a Showroom Admission Card and (his or her) spouse and children are permitted to make purchases with the card. Any abuses or misrepresentation of this privilege will result in revocation.

3. Best Products reserves the right to refuse showroom privileges to anyone when, in the opinion

Within the image:

BEST
PRODUCTS

1974
BUYER'S
BOOK
NUMBER
117

GIFTS, PRIZES,
INCENTIVE AWARDS.

DIAMONDS   TOYS
WATCHES   CHINA
SPORTING GOODS   RADIOS
JEWELRY   CLOCKS
LUGGAGE   CAMERAS
LEATHER GOODS   PHONOGRAPHS
APPLIANCES   EVERYTHING FOR
SILVERWARE   THE HOME.

CALIFORNIA—Sacramento / MARYLAND—Baltimore,
Carrollton, Rockville / MICHIGAN—Flint / NORTH
CAROLINA—Durham, Fayetteville, Raleigh / OHIO—
Akron, Dayton, Parma (Cleveland), Toledo, Willowick
(Cleveland) / TEXAS—Amarillo, Austin, Corpus
Christi, Dallas, Houston, Lubbock, San Antonio,
Wichita Falls / VIRGINIA—Arlington, Falls
Church, Hampton, Lynchburg, Richmond,
Roanoke, Virginia Beach.

FIGURE 19 Cover of the Best catalog. This is a "buyer's book," which means that it is for purchasing agents and marketing directors looking for incentive sales awards as well as for the regular family market.

Best Buyer's Book: The Catalog of many uses.

Retail Dealers.

Introducing your most colorful new counter salesman. Display this catalog prominently and let us sell merchandise for you. A complete range of nationally advertised merchandise is now available to your customers, but without inventory or capital investment from you. Who could ask for more?

Incentives and Awards.

Here's a proven way to stimulate sales, safety, efficiency and most any other company program that might need a boost. Use the catalog for a broad selection of merchandise for incentives. Anniversaries, outstanding achievements, and

Personnel Managers.

Many businesses offer the use of this catalog to their employees. The substantial savings they get goes a long way towards building employee morale. Additional catalogs will be furnished to your company on request.

Non-profit Organizations.

Civic groups, churches, fraternal organizations are among the many who have found the Best Catalog to be possibly the best source from which to select merchandise for fund-raising and similar projects. We take pride in a long list of groups we have served in this way.

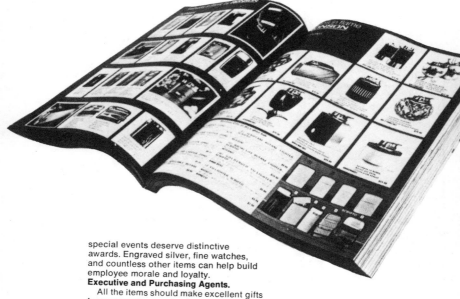

special events deserve distinctive awards. Engraved silver, fine watches, and countless other items can help build employee morale and loyalty.

Executive and Purchasing Agents.

All the items should make excellent gifts for your customers, business associates or employees. Add the personal touch to many items with engraving or stamping in quantity.

FIGURE 20 The second page of the Best Buyer's Book, which explains to the reader the "many uses."

of the management, it is not in the best interest of Best Products Co.

The card also has a line: "this is a showroom purchase card—not a credit card." In the Tiffany & Co. Annual Report, dated March 20, 1973, on the other hand, the Chairman mentions that while their approximately 110,000 regular charge customers continued to receive the catalog free, all others were charged one dollar, which approximately covered the costs involved. This enabled them to offer the catalog to prospective customers by advertising it in national magazines and in local newspapers in cities where they have stores. "By January 31st" (the Chairman, Walter Hoving, continues) "over 40,000 requests were filled." Mr. Hoving states that the Tiffany catalog is not just a Christmas catalog but a year-round publication. Best is not without the best competition.

Other competition to Best and the DCS formula are some attempts to bring in the shop-by-phone technique, which has been tested in the United States and other countries. A Best manager mentioned that he felt this type of shopping could be done in the future in his store. Illinois Bell Telephone has connected their Picturephone service between one of Bonwit Teller's Chicago branches and eight other local retailers. The system costs $86.50 per month and includes 25 to 30 minutes of free calling time. Bonwit merchandise is viewed on one of the 325 or so Picturephone sets in the Chicago area.

Some More Best Forms. Best has a form for charge sales that includes the statement of terms, which are net 10 days, as well as firm name, address, city and state, "your name," account number, code, and purchase order number; and for the store to fill in, location, sold by, picked by, date, complete catalog number, how many, article, coded price, and amount. Best allows returns within ten days, but all returned merchandise must be accompanied by the sales receipt and the original carton and packing material. This information is also on this form. This form, like other Best forms, has multiple copies —one for EDP, billing, invoice, customer, and warehouse. There is a drop shipper form with similar information for customer, office, and warehouse. The forms mentioned here are not meant to be inclusive, but they are outstanding and worth studying.

Other Best Activities. Best provides film mailers for their catalog film club with their low coded price and a 15-cents-off coupon. Their service is advertised as 24 to 48 hour rush in plant. Costs and time to the customer are both very attractive.

Store Hours. Best is again a good guide for most of the industry. During the week the store hours are 9:30 A.M. to 9:00 P.M. On Saturday, the hours are 9:30 A.M. to 6:00 P.M. During the Christmas season, there are extended hours (usually from the first of November until Christmas eve or December 22 or 23, depending on the day of the week on which Christmas eve falls). Then, hours are from 9:30 A.M. to 9:00 P.M. The 9:00 P.M. also includes Saturday, but not Sunday. Not all areas permit (or require) Sunday openings.

The Best Lookout. According to the May 7, 1973, issue of *Discount Store News,* the Best acquisition of the two-store Levy & Sons catalog showroom chain was worth an extra $3 million in volume for Best. With that and the profit picture for overall best showroom operations, it seems that the pioneer is still forging ahead. Smith,

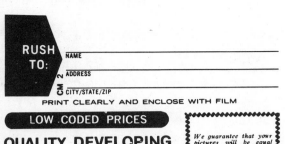

FIGURE 21 Best's film mailer. Rates and a money-saving coupon are on back. Best guarantees the quality of the photographs.

Barney and Company say that Best has a young organization with a strong position.

Inflation will take the present figures up somewhat, too. The Best TRU-specials on many items may mean some reduction of margins for the company, but it is hard to say how much this will be affected because they have not revealed the percentage markdowns. However, after studying the "reductions" for the catalog ending May 26, 1973, it is easy to say that the TRU-special prices are significantly lower than Best's regular prices. For example, a deluxe riding mower at their usual price of $418.97 was marked down to $389.87 (list is $625.00). Even jewelry is substantially reduced. However, on some items, there is a limited-quantity notice. With all these reductions, Best is still coming on strong. Can you imagine what their profit would be without them?

Modern Merchandising, Inc. The annual report, dated September 1, 1972, shows tremendous growth for this company. Sales were 75 percent greater in 1972 than 1971—up to $40,775,000. In fiscal year 1973 they were $90 million. Some 90 percent of this came from the showrooms. Net earnings were up to $1,371,359 in 1972 from $725,000 in 1971. The catalog division, Creative Merchandising, is expected to increase catalog production and sales (to 40 merchandise companies) from 5.2 million in 1973 to 8 million catalogs in 1974. The major Modern Merchandising divisions are:

- LaBelle's catalog showrooms in Denver
- Anchor Distributing (showrooms) in the St. Louis Area
- Dixie Wholesale (showrooms) in New Orleans

- Standard Sales (showrooms) in Tallahassee and Jacksonville
- King Distributors (showrooms) in Tampa
- Great Western Distributing in Lewiston, Idaho
- Phil Miller (showrooms) in Canton, Ohio
- Rogers Distributing in Grand Rapids
- JAFCO and Creative Merchandising catalog publishers

Dain, Kalman & Quail (100 Dain Tower, Minneapolis, Minn.) has published a *FOCUS* research report on Modern Merchandising in 1972.

Gaylord's National announced its first catalog showroom for Washington, Pennsylvania. It will have 25,000 square feet total space, and the showroom will have 11,000 square feet of this space. They will use the Jewelcor catalog. Their second unit, Tower—Jewelers and Distributors, will open in Dover, Delaware, with 11,000 square feet.

Cook United (in Cleveland and the Midwest) is to open two DCS units to add to its 100-store SSDDS chain.

Robertson and Ruth, Ogden Avenue, Downers Grove, Ohio, is opening its second unit of 50,000 square feet. The company is an 18-year old veteran of the discount catalog showroom line.

Super Valu continues its expansion plan. This voluntary chain—supermarkets, SSDDS—group plans DCS units in Green Bay, Appleton, and Menahsa, Wisconsin. They will be part of the ShopKo division.

And there are more:

- Goldbro's is in Birmingham
- H. B. Davis Co. is based in Hartford, Connecticut
- Sam Gordon is in Madison, New Jersey
- Green Shield opened on July 21, 1973, in Great Britain under the name Argos—this company is owned by the principals of one of the largest trading stamp companies in G.B.
- Carlson has seven DCS units and catalog desks within its Piggly Wiggly supermarkets
- Belscot will have a DCS division operating within Belscot discount stores; they will use the DLI coordinators
- FedMart and Clarkins will try out catalogs

Our Canadian Cousins. Returning a moment to Canada; there is good DCS activity north of our border. Cardinal is a division of Steinberg's Miracle Mart and has 14 units in operation, and planned to have 35 by the end of 1973 and then 20 more in 1974. Shop-Rite is a division of Hudson's Bay Company and has 35 units. Acme is a Neonex division with 23 units. Woolco planned 9 or 10 units for 1973 as a part of F. W. Woolworth's expansion. Their first DCS units are converted Woolworth variety stores.

More About Catalogs and Coordinators

As we discussed in Chapter 2, DCS catalogs are very similar to each other because they are prepared by catalog coordinators, and because operators would want to carry similar merchandise. However, different catalog coordinators put different emphasis on merchandise categories. Also, individual showrooms or chains have the opportunity, to varying extents, to customize their catalogs. Because of these factors, the number of pages devoted to specific merchandise varies from book to book. Following is a listing of the page-count and category breakdown for nine coordinator catalogs. Please note that these page counts are not exact for the reason given here already: different companies make individual changes, so all books produced by these coordinators may not have these exact space allocations. This chart compares the Creative catalog use by Best, Mutual's used by Martin's, Comprehensive's used by Tulkian, MAI's used by H.B. Davis, and Jewelcor's used by GEX.

How Catalogers Allocate Pages in Their Books

	Bell	Creative	Giant Food	Mutual	Ellman's	Comprehensive	MAI	United	Jewelcor
Sterling Holloware	16	5	3	4½	5	4	2½	2	2
Silverplated Holloware	33	21	10	19	21	12	11	14	14
Sterling Flatware	4	4	4	4	1	2	3	1	3
Silverplated Flatware	2½	1	0	1	⅓	1	0	0	0
Stainless Flatware	4	4	4	3	2⅓	1	3	2	2
Diamond Engagement Rings	10	7	10	11	10	13	10	8	14½
Other Ladies' Jewelry	49	59	49	57	60	58	40½	45	70
Men's Jewelry	9	14	9	16	10	12	8	12	9
Men's Watches	10	14½	9	12	13	7	9	11	12
Ladies' Watches	13	15½	11	12	17	17	18	14	14

Clocks	8	14	6	12	10	6	13	6	13
Ladies' Giftware	7	12	6	11½	20	4½	12	9	9
Ladies' Handbags/Billfolds	4	4	1	5	2	1	2	1	2
Men's Wallets	3	3½	1	3	4	1	4	3	3
Men's Giftware	6	11½	2½	13	12	3½	9	7	5
Bar Accessories and Bars	6	8	1	6½	6	3	9	7	5½
Brief & Attache Cases	3	2	0	1	1½		3	½	2
Luggage & Trunks	7	9	4	7	8	4	12	4½	8
Desk Accessories & Pens	4	5	4	3	9½	1½	5	5½	2½
Smokers' Accessories	2	5	2	4	4	1½	2	2	4
Typewriters & Office Machines	3	4½	2½	5	3	1	3	2	1½
Binocs, Telescopes, Microscopes	3	4	1½	3	4	2	3	3	3
Cameras & Accessories	6	14	4	14½	11½	3	23	9	8
Decorator Accessories	5	2	½	10	14⅔	2	16	5	9½

	Bell	Creative	Giant Food	Mutual	Ellman's	Comprehensive	MAI	United	Jewelcor
Barometers, etc.	1½	2	1	2	2½	1	2	1	1
Televisions	2	4½	3	3	3	1	4	2	3½
Radios	4	13	8	8	9	3½	10	10	7
Phonos—Tapes—Hi-Fi Sets	7	18	7	15	20	4	19	9	9
China, Dinnerware	4½	1½	2	1	1	0	2	½	2
Ironstone Dinnerware	½	2	1	3	3	1	3	1	3
Crystal	10	2	3	4	4	1	2	3	3
Gourmet & Cookware	6	11	11	11	10	3	12	5½	6½
Appliances	13	28	19½	31	21½	12½	40	20½	18½
Wood Giftware	6	9	0	5½	5½	2	5	4	6½
Cutlery	3	5	3	3	2	2	3	1	2½

Cutting Acces.—Barbecues	1	2	2	0	1	½	3	3	2
Camping Equipment	3½	5	6	0	3	3	4	7	2
Blankets, Bedspreads, Towels	1	0	2	⅓	3	2	7	2	2
Fireplace Equipment	0	½	1	0	1	1½	0	2	1
Furniture (Folding, Carts, etc.)	4	3	9	1	6	6½	5½	8	3
Musical Instruments	½	0	3	0	4	3	3	4	1
Beauty & Health Appliances	8	6	18	2⅔	8	8	3	10	2
Baby Furnishings	9	10	14	1	5	4	6	11	⅔
Bicycles—Tricycles, etc.	1½	2	4	0	1	2	9	3	1⅓
Sporting Goods	19½	19	20	0	11	9½	37	20	5
Games & Toys	40½	38	31	0	19	6	6½	53	4
Power Tools, Hand Tools	3	0	15	0	5	4	1	8	2
Pewter	1	¼	0	1	1	3	1	1	3

Source: *Discount Store News*, Vol. 12, No. 16 (July 30, 1973), p. 34.

The Last Words

To end, a statement from the beginning could be repeated: The catalog showroom will do well because it combines features of the catalog and the service as well as the self-service store. Look back at the last three decades. And earlier. The supermarket really got self-service into every formula during the Depression because of necessity. Until that time, people still desired 10-cents worth of service on a 10-cent can of peas.

On the other hand, the stores that are *too mechanical* fail and have failed. The customer still wants to see, to feel, to pick up, and to put back if not finally desired. The DCS permits all this. Self-service permits all this, too, but the DCS offers a hint of the futuristic just as the 1945 Keedoozle store did for Clarence Saunders, the founder and ex-president of Piggly Wiggly Stores. In the Keedoozle store, the customer carried a type of "key" that was inserted into locks in cases containing the merchandise. A conveyor system carried the merchandise from the stock room to the checkout, where the order was identified by the "key" number, and where the merchandise was paid for and picked up by the customer. There have been other punched-card systems, and all of these could work well if:

- The customer could feel the merchandise, yet put it back if so desired.

- The price was low enough to take the romance out of the shopping trip and replace it with dollar savings.

This last is an important point: The customer still wants service and nicely appointed, exciting stores, but not if she has to pay for them. So far, this has not happened. Too much romance has been taken out and the prices are *not that low*. However, the DCS price is low, and there is some romance remaining in the display and in the system. The mechanical part has a long way to go. There are tests being conducted that make shopping less romantic: you dial your computer number to connect you with the wholesaler, manufacturer, or retailer, and moments later you have the merchandise at your door. This is really *no romance*. However, the supermarket came with depression, the automatic system could come with inflation. An in-between could be the large warehouse stores. With 200,000 square feet of selling space, it is a warehouse. Levitz is a warehouse store, but for food and other items there is no need for a showroom. Let the customers pick up the merchandise directly from the warehouse. Another step is eliminated from the Levitz system (or maybe two steps, if the showroom is removed). The DCS is an in-between, too. It is succeeding and will continue to succeed because it combines all the best features of our wonderful and highly efficient distribution system.

But . . . The Pitfalls

Mr. Jerome Kaufman,[1] the president of the newly

[1] Mr. Kaufman is Managing Director of Mutual Merchandising Co-op, which turns out 3.5 million catalogs of 300 pages. Mutual prints a 220 page and also a 400 page catalog for companies such as Summit Gift Gallery. Mutual's competition includes Creative Merchandising (division of Modern Merchandising Corp.) which prints some 5 million catalogs plus supplements for about

formed National Association of Catalog Showroom Merchandisers, gives no exact figures on how the scorecard will read. No one can. It is truly an expanding, dynamic industry, this discount catalog showroom.

Families, retail dealers, personnel managers, nonprofit organizations, executives, and purchasing agents, TAKE NOTE: The discount catalog showroom can still be entered, and by you. However (and a *big* however), up to now, we have mainly discussed what you *should* do. Here are some of the things that you should *not* do, and these are things that people who learned the hard way are warning newcomers about:

1. Do not open in an overpopulated (store population), already competitive area, at least not until you really know the ropes.

2. When you do open, make sure your fast expansion is not overexpansion, and make sure you are not underfinanced.

3. Learn the cyclical nature of the business, and be prepared for the lean months, which are in the beginning of every calendar year. This is very important. Because a lot of emphasis is on gift-type items, most of your business will be Christmas business—in fact probably about 45 to 65 percent of it is.[2] If you try to advertise

---

a $6 million volume. Creative serves 160 showrooms and 36 firms. Best is Creative's customer (see Best in charts) with 750,000 catalogs in 1973 and 1,500,000 in 1974. Progressive Buying Association is another competitor who serves 178 firms, which are small and average about $500,000 a year. Progressive publishes a 300 page catalog but custom tailors it from 240 up to 600 pages.

[2] *Discount Store News,* July 30, 1973, p. 13.

during these lean months to boost sales, you will be losing the already small margins you have.

4. Untrained and inexperienced management with too little energy to make up the difference is a great hazard. You love your uncle, but does he know what he's doing?

5. Almost as an adjunct to number 4, do not enter a field that relies heavily on diamond and other jewelry sales for profits (even though electronics are catching up, this is still number one across the boards) without the necessary jewelry merchandising expertise, or without someone who does have it.

6. Do not rely too readily on the advice and sales talks of the coordinators—they want to sell their catalogs. Thank them and think about it. New fields tie up capital, as you well know, and this generally bearish period is giving everyone sagging profits.

7. Watch history and avoid the discounters' early problems: overbuying and overstocking. This should be scientific in this age of computers.

8. Watch the innovations—not-in-catalog goods are a great help to regionalizing your unit, but they also mean extra ordering, stocking, and display time, and therefore extra money. Also, it is one thing to sell with the help of a very carefully merchandised book, and another to make merchandising decisions on your own. You need skill *and* space. Will your coordinator help you purchase these goods? Are they really keeping your customers happy and helping your margins? Also, advertising and promotional markdowns

are necessary, but not to any great extent. The normally low prices used to be more than sufficient to undersell the discounters, and the one, always-low price was a strong selling point for the DCS. If you start in with discounters' methods, you are losing a basic principle of catalog selling. These innovations also tear away valuable margins. Jewelcor believes in not-in-catalog merchandise, but remember that Jewelcor is one of the biggies—they have been around long enough to afford experiments.

9. Do not over-promote an item or merchandise group in the catalog to bolster sales. The percentage of the catalog devoted to each category should be proportional to the category's percentage of sales. Giving more room to something does not mean you will sell more of it. Catalog pages are precious.

Some More Pitfalls: We have been warned that the life cycle of the new discount catalog showrooms could only be seven years until full maturity is reached. Changes in postal rates could cause the policy of sending out catalogs as the advertising medium to be shifted. If the DCS decides to fight other forms of retailing on a conventional battleground (including newspaper advertising), much of its advantage will be lost.

The following from the Wall Street Journal of November 5, 1964, indicates that traditional catalog companies (Sears, Montgomery Ward, Spiegel, and the latecomer J. C. Penney) have been thinking about ways to expand for almost 10 years. Imagine the share of the market these giants could capture.

Sears, Ward Boost Sales in Small Towns By Franchising Stores.

'Ma and Pa' Catalog Units Cut Costs, Offer Speedy Service; Minister Takes in $150,000.

TRACY, Minn.—Last April, Edson Starr and his wife, Catherine, opened a new store in this little southern Minnesota town. The Starrs didn't need to invest much money nor did they need much experience in retailing. For all the merchandise and advice they can use is being supplied free.

The supplier is Montgomery Ward & Co. which has franchised the Starrs to run a catalog store where customers can order from Ward's huge catalog and pick up their merchandise later. Ward and Sears, Roebuck & Co. have been franchising similar outlets in small towns around the country at great speed.

Both giant retail chains regard *the franchise stores as an economical answer to their long quest for something better than mail order selling in small towns and rural areas.* In the past these big catalog firms have tried, with little success, such things as enlisting the county agricultural agent's wife to drum up customer interest in person and over the phone. Now, Ward says, it can often triple or quadruple the sales volume from a town by franchising a catalog store there.

The franchised operations are run by people working for themselves not by employes of the chain as in the catalog stores long familiar to city shoppers. Usually the franchise holders are husband and wife teams who are relatively new to the retail field. Even so they often can produce a profit for the company in a town which is not big enough to support a regular catalog unit, with its salaried employes.

Racing for Sites

Since Jan. 1 Ward has opened 88 of its franchised "catalog sales agencies" from New York to Oregon and expects to push this figure to 144 within the next three months. Ward figures there are more than 2,000 counties in the U.S. which have at least one town suitable for a franchised catalog store. Sears now has some 60 "catalog sales merchants" and while the company won't discuss its franchise operations, competitors says Sears is racing Ward for sites and franchise holders in suitable towns.

The Starrs' store in this town of about 3,000 people is typical of the operations franchised by both chains. Over the front swings a bright red and white Ward sign, which along with the lights, counters and other standard fixtures, were supplied free to the Starrs by Ward.

Most orders are placed through the catalogs the Starrs keep stacked on the counter. But lined up around the store are such items as washers, dryers, ranges, tires, batteries, snow throwers, and water heaters, all for sale and all furnished by Ward on consignment to the Starrs. The Starrs pay no franchise fee, only the rent on the store, utility bills and other overhead. They receive 8% of sales revenue as gross income.

"How else can a couple go into business with more than 130,000 items of merchandise and not a cent of capital," says William Davis, who runs a Ward's catalog store in Sleepy Eye, Minn.

Cost Percentages

For the most efficient operations, catalog men say, expenses for the franchise holder only amount to about 1% of total volume. In such operations "ma" watches the store while "pa" does outside selling of home improvement products and carpeting. In stores where the franchise holders employ outside help, expenses often run about 3% of volume.

Industry sources estimate that franchised catalog stores need to produce about $100,000 a year in sales volume to be successful. Many already are doing better than that. Max Fisk, a Baptist minister who gave up his congregation for a Sears franchise in St. Croix Falls, Wis., a town of 1,250 people, reports he did $150,000 worth of business last year and expects to hit $195,000 this year. In Forest Lake Minn., population 2,300, the Sears franchise holder says his store grossed $138,000 last year and figures it will take in $175,000 this year.

Franchised stores are helped by the fact that through their catalogs they can offer 130,000 to 150,000 items, far more than local small town retailers can stock. They generally can have these items on hand within 48 hours, because they are regularly serviced by Ward's and Sears' trucks and this pickup service is almost always cheaper for the customer than having goods mailed or shipped to him. What's more, the two big chains can offer shoppers more generous credit terms than are usually available from local retailers.

As important as all this is to the success of franchise stores are the husband and wife teams who run them. They usually have lived most of their lives in the community and have the trust and friendship of most citizens. Also, because they are working for themselves they're likely to be more energetic and enthusiastic than anyone Sears or Ward could hire.

"Out of personal conversations on children, illnesses, animals and the weather, with no sign of the traditional merchandising techniques, these home town people can sell a lot of merchandise," says James Gilbertson, who manages Ward's franchised operations for the Minneapolis area. "Placing a professional company-trained manager from another city in these same little towns would usually be a waste of time."

The catalog companies usually locate candidates for their franchises by advertising and by following leads of local civic leaders. The relative ease of checking on a resident of a small community helps the big catalog companies safeguard their reputations in the franchise field.

"We spent almost a century building up the Ward name, so naturally we have great concern as to who gets a Ward franchise," says Charles F. Higgins, Ward's catalog merchandise manager. "But after almost a year of expereince, we have no concern now that they don't represent us as well as our own people in other units."

Once selected, a Ward franchise holder gets about two weeks of training in the rudiments of selling in a company-owned catalog store. He's then assigned a "big brother" on the chain's management staff whom he can call to discuss problems.

Clearly the franchise stores spell tough new competition for small town retailers. But some local officials argue that the addition of such stores helps little towns hold their own against bigger neighboring cities with major stores.

A third big chain store and mail order firm, Gamble-Skogmo, Inc., is understood to be planning to plunge into franchised catalog stores as soon as it completes the purchase of Aldens, Inc., another mail order house. J. C. Penney Co. officials say only that they are "watching" their competitors' franchise ventures. Spiegel, Inc., officials term the franchise stores "interesting" but say they plan to expand further into metropolitan areas before trying them.

Catalog Stores are Facing Employee Problems and Pilferage Costs. Polygraph tests are being given (and complained about). Unions have protested and pickets have been formed by employees. So far, however, employees are highly motivated, and personnel problems are not what they are in other retail fields, not yet, anyway.

And Hasty Moves Risky. More pitfalls are pointed out by the following article:

CATALOG SHOWROOMS TO GO ROUTE OF DISCOUNT STORES. Grow rapidly through mid-1970s. Lose competitive edge as expansion dilutes uniqueness, increases overhead. Showroom sales to grow estimated 17% a year to $5.7 billion by 1978. Compared to discount store sales of $33 billion for 1972 (up 10%). Discounters squeezed by customers' demand for quality, service along with insistence on low price. Catalog showrooms keep prices down by concentration on high-demand items, low overhead, elimination of opportunities for pilferage. Department stores, discount chains attracted to catalog business by current growth, ease of entry. Vornado Inc., Giant Stores Corp. open showrooms. Jewelcor Inc., W.T. Grant Co. plan cooperative operation of 30 Granjewel showrooms. Hasty moves risky. Rapid expansion of Supermarkets General's Value House showrooms (five new outlets last year, six more planned for 1973) reduced 1972 profits 7.7% despite 85% rise in sales to $34.6 million. Attraction of showrooms' uniqueness already on wane. Large operators turn to non-catalog special sales to generate traffic.[3]

Back to *The Last Words,* before the pitfalls: And why is retailing and distribution in general so great in the United States? Yes, everyone knows that it can cost 25 cents to buy that 5 cent apple these days. But are you willing to return to those good old days of 70-hour work

[3] "The Gallagher Report," July 9, 1973, p. 2. Published by The Gallagher Report, Inc., © 1973. Reprinted by permission.

weeks with $5.00 per week in your pocket? It all lies in the percentage count, folks. Think for a moment. Where else do food and the necessities cost so little as a *percentage* of disposable income? Yes, it is the only country in the world, *even today*, where the poor have a parking problem and color television. (A little exaggerated, maybe, but you get my point.)

Distribution is very efficient, but this is the reason why we need to investigate and test more automation, more computerization, more mechanization so that we can get that apple back to 5 cents and still pay everyone $5.00 per hour for that 32-hour week and still have a return on investment of 15 percent or more. Good luck to us all. We got the man on the moon . . . we can get the bacon on the table.

About the Author

J. M. de Bernardi has been with National Cash Register since 1955 and is now Seminar Coordinator for the International MMM (Management and Merchandising Methods) Seminars. He was previously with Federated Department Stores (Rikes Division) for five years, where he served as a part-time credit supervisor.

Mr. de Bernardi is also the editor of the *MMM News* and MMM *Facts* as well as other NRC publications on distribution. He writes articles for *Sales Manager Bulletin* here in the United States, and for *Succes* (Netherlands) and *CO-OP* (Switzerland). His recent articles this year have been on MBO (management by objectives) and retail trends.

Always on the go, Mr. de Bernardi is a lecturer on

distribution and management trends at conventions, seminars, and conferences in the United States, Australia, New Zealand, Scotland, France, The Netherlands, Sweden, Denmark, Austria, China, The Philippines, Ecuador, and Colombia. He has also lectured at the University of Dayton, Adelaide University, and Monash University (Melbourne, Australia). To do all this, he is making, on the average, four trips to Europe and one to Latin America, Australia, and Asia each year. He also visits major retailers and important store openings in the United States and Canada in order to study and report on stores and distribution operations.

The author got his B.A. degree in International Relations at Southern Illinois University, and got an M.A. in the same field at Georgetown University. He also has an M.B.A. degree in Management from the University of Dayton. His education also includes Ph.D. course work in Management at the University of Cincinnati, and a Russian language course at the University of Tennessee.

Born in Glenridge, Illinois, the author now lives with his wife in Dayton, Ohio. There, he is an active Rotarian. He was formerly a member of the United States Junior Chamber of Commerce and the Jaycees International. He has received special awards for meritorious service from the U.S. Army Medical Corps and the Citizenship Medal from the Danforth Foundation.

Other Business Builders
from Chain Store Publishing Corporation

Belden, Don, *The Role of the Buyer in Mass Merchandising*

Bolt Beranek & Newman, *Today's Busboy*

Bolt Beranek & Newman, *Today's Cocktail Waitress*

Bolt Beranek & Newman, *Today's Dishwashing Machine Operator*

Bolt Beranek & Newman, *Today's Waitress*

Bryan, John R., *Turning Food Service Into Profits: A Personnel Handbook for Restaurant Operators*

Chisholm, Robert F., *The Darlings: The Mystique of the Supermarket*

Clevenger, Charles, *Market Profile 1970*

Curtis, Bob, *Security Control: External Theft*

Curtis, Bob, *Security Control: Internal Theft*

Degenshein, Joan, and Naomi Manners Stern, *Successful Cosmetic Selling*

Fulweiler, John H., *How to Promote Your Shopping Center*

German, Gene A., *In-Basket Program for Management Trainees*

Harwell, Edward M., *Checkout Management*

Harwell, Edward M., *Personnel Management and Training*

Kahrl, William L., *Planning and Operating a Successful Food Service Operation*

Kaylin, S. O., *Understanding Today's Food Warehouse*

Lebhar, Godfrey M., *Chain Stores in America*

Lebhar, Godfrey M., *The Use of Time*

Leed, Theodore W., and Gene A. German, *Food Merchandising: Principles and Practices*

Mallowe, Charles A., and Daniel J. McLaughlin, Jr., *Food Marketing and Distribution: Selected Readings*

Mitchell, Glenn E., and Edward M. Harwell, *Leadership Appraisal*

Moseley, Lloyd W., *Customer Service: The Road to Greater Profits*

Padberg, Daniel I., *Today's Food Broker: Vital Link in the Distribution Cycle*

Paulson, R. Lee, *The Computer Challenge in Retailing*

Pinto, David, *How to Make Ecology Work for You*